McCoy, You're Going Straight to Hell

Heartfelt Letters to a Gay State Senator
on Marriage Equality

by

Iowa State Senator Matt McCoy

&

Jim Ferguson

Michael —
Best Wishes
in NY — Hope
you are part of
the civil rights
cause.
Matt McCoy
J Ferguson

"McCoy, You're Going Straight to Hell - Heartfelt Letters to a Gay State Senator on Marriage Equality," by Matt McCoy and Jim Ferguson

Front cover image by Ben Easter.

ISBN 978-1-62137-626-2 (Softcover) 978-1-62137-627-9 (Ebook)

for

~

my son

Jack McCoy

~

my wife

Jill Ferguson

Table of Contents

About the Authors...i

Preface iv

Chapter 1: Truth is Out and So am I 5

Chapter 2: No Longer Second Class Citizens 19

Chapter 3: Your Personal Views Are Not Relevant — LET US VOTE!..41

Chapter 4: Saint or Sinner McCoy, You Will Be Accountable to GOD for this ONE! 91

Chapter 5: Social Media Gone Wild............................. 121

Chapter 6: Targeted Mass Communication 129

Chapter 7: Watch Your Back — we know where you live 139

Chapter 8: Post 4/09–The Fight for Justice Continues ... 157

Appendices.. 179

Acknowledgements 197

Bibliography... 199

About the Authors

Ferguson—Introducing Matt McCoy:

The first things you notice about Matt are his engaging smile and good looks. His congenial exterior belies a complex individual. Highly intelligent he serves in leadership positions at the Iowa Senate which includes handling controversial bills and complicated tasks. Well dressed and immaculate, he is at ease with all. People seek him out at the Capitol, in restaurants, at events, in stores, and at church. They may be offering support or requesting assistance. Regardless, he listens and has a pleasant comment or compliment, or if appropriate, a resolution.

Iowa State Senator Matt McCoy's popularity is reflected in his never having lost an election. He has served a total of 22 years at the Iowa State House in the House of Representatives and Senate. He is Iowa's highest ranking, openly gay elected official. When he came out eleven years ago, he was the only openly gay person in the Capitol. Now there is one other whose sexuality has never made headlines due in part to Matt's pioneering the way for others to be open about their sexual orientation.

The impact of Matt's work in the Senate can be seen throughout the Des Moines metro area and state. Housing, flood re-building, public transportation, and urban renewal projects will create his legacy. Matt is chair of the Senate Commerce Committee and also chair of the Transportation, Infrastructure, and Capitals Appropriations Committee. He serves as Assistant Majority Leader in the Iowa Senate.

Matt is well known in Democratic politics. He's a spokesperson on marriage equality at the state and national levels. *NY Times*, *Time Magazine*, etc. have quoted him. The *Des Moines Register* quotes him regularly. He was invited and presented at an international conference on HIV in Australia.

Matt is actively involved in the Victory Fund where he has spoken at numerous national events.

Matt's leadership extends into his community, Des Moines. His membership on numerous charitable boards provides venues for him to give back to the community and influence its future. Numerous organizations throughout the State have honored him with their annual awards recognizing his contributions in areas of social justice, assistance to the homeless, support for those in need of special assistance, and for furthering the general welfare of its citizens.

State legislators are citizen legislators meaning their work at the State House is not intended to be a full time job. Thus, all but the retired have jobs in their other life. Resource Development Consultants was begun by Matt to seek funding for non-profits and build their capacity. In addition, he renovates houses for re-sale.

Because Matt wears many hats simultaneously he is a master at multi-tasking. But always there is time for his son Jack — attending school activities, going on fishing trips, skiing at Christmas or popcorn and movies at home. While divorced, Matt and his former wife maintain a close and supportive relationship. They are all active members in Plymouth Congregational Church in Des Moines. Everyone addresses Senator McCoy simply as "Matt". That says a lot.

McCoy—Introducing Jim Ferguson:

Jim is an intense man with a twinkle in his eye and a great sense of fun. He's intelligent, energetic, assertive, and a tireless worker. He looks for results. He is retired after a career as a teacher, public school administrator, college instructor, and teacher of teachers. He is the author of numerous publications. A community activist, he has focused on obtaining support for the homeless and less fortunate.

Jim and I met during John Kerry's 2004 Presidential Campaign. That year he also assisted me on my campaign for the Iowa Senate. Later he worked closely with me as I battled federal charges of extortion. The trial ended with the jury taking only minutes to find me not guilty. Jim then joined me at the Senate as my clerk. We continue to work together in my firm Resource Development Consultants.

During the time Jim worked in the Senate, marriage equality was (and continues to be) a hot topic. E-mails poured in. As Jim collected them for my review, we realized these were original artifacts on a crucial human rights issue. As such, the stories they related should be preserved. Thus, the birth of *McCoy, You're Going Straight to Hell.*

Jim's position on marriage equality evolved over time which is probably true of many of our readers. The first stage was one of indifference — why would two people of the same gender want to get married? Why do they make a big deal out of it? They only have to look at the current divorce rates and ask why would they want to be part of that? He identifies stage two as not understanding why marriage unions weren't enough? Stage three was an understanding that marriage equality is the new civil rights and understanding the depth of commitment that marriage brings to a relationship. That evolution took years and the e-mails presented in this book played an important role in his transitioning.

Jim has been married for forty years to the former Jill Deskin. Jim and Jill are members and actively involved in Plymouth Congregational Church and St. Paul's Episcopal Cathedral. They enjoy time spent with their two granddaughters. His marriage has fostered an understanding of why same gender couples would want to experience the same expression of love and depth of total commitment. He feels there is no other bond in the world like it.

Preface

On August 30, 2007, Polk County District Court Judge Hansen ruled the statute (Iowa Code section 595.2) limiting civil marriage to a union between a man and a woman was unconstitutional under the due process and equal protection clauses of the Iowa Constitution. The court reaffirmed that a statute inconsistent with the Iowa Constitution must be declared void, even though it may be supported by strong and deep-seated traditional beliefs and popular opinion.

Although the Polk County District Court's decision was to allow six gay couples to marry, they were refused to be given marriage licenses by the Polk County Recorder under current Iowa law. A motion for a stay was made by the Polk County Attorney which was granted.

April 3, 2009 Iowa became the third state in the nation, and the first in the mid-west, to allow same sex marriages. By an unanimous decision, the Iowa Supreme Court declared in a landmark ruling that the Iowa statute (Iowa Code section 595.2) limiting civil marriage to a union between a man and a woman violates the equal protection clause of the Iowa Constitution.

Chapter 1: Truth is Out and So am I

"I was living history. I was actually making history as we moved forward with equality for all."

~ Iowa State Senator Matt McCoy

I'm an Iowa State Senator.

I'm gay, and I'm openly gay.

Prior to my coming out, gay Massachusetts Congressional Representative Barney Frank told me that when I come out, "It will be the most important decision of your life. You'll never feel better and nobody else will give a damn." I've never felt freer.

My journey toward self-acceptance has been the toughest in my life — it's been pure hell. The wreckage along the way has been painful for those whom I love as well as for me.

I'm free at last to be me.

That freedom has been exhilarating.

Eliminating all forms of discrimination is a non-ending struggle. Marriage equality is at the forefront of the current battle to extend civil liberties to all. *McCoy, You're Going Straight to Hell* relates not only my story but shares the stories and views of individuals who have been impacted by the intolerance of laws preventing them from legally expressing their love and commitment through marriage. On the other side of this issue, it also tells the stories of individuals who feel threatened by its legalization. Together, these stories put a face on marriage equality which humanizes the issue. Marriage validates a relationship unlike any other commitment. Through these stories raw emotion is sensed. By reading these stories you too may become a champion of marriage equality and continue the quest for equal rights for everyone. You will begin to see the writers of these stories as real people not as labels. If not, I hope you'll at least understand the depth of feelings of those impacted. These stories are told through e-mails sent to me at the Iowa State Senate as I fought to challenge inequality and to fight for justice for all, not just for some.

Marriage equality — same gender marriage — is the new civil rights movement. Through my personal story, along with the hundreds of heartfelt e-mails which I received, the impact of the struggle for marriage equality will become obvious. It is my hope that these personal narratives will empower others in similar circumstance to have the courage to face, accept, and celebrate their own sexuality and relationships. It is my hope that this celebration will inspire the continued battle for full equality.

Personal stories shared and differing views on marriage equality bring a sense of humanity to the critical issues faced by same-sex couples. Stories demonstrate the complications created during life threatening illnesses, relationships gone sour, and end-of-life decisions, that marriage equality resolves. The stress and fear of coming out of the closet is part of these testimonies. Stories have freed individuals from having to hide who they truly are, from masking the central core of their identity. Personal narratives empower others sharing a similar fate to come out of the shadows.

Found between the covers of this book are highly personal stories. It is my story and those of others who have struggled with their sexual identification. We all have traveled the same journey experiencing agony, fear, and desperation.

Sharing my story has been painful as I relived memories blocked for self-preservation. I've come to terms with my past. I am who I am. My cherished privacy seems a small price to pay when I have the opportunity — nah, the obligation — to reach out to help others come to terms with their own sexuality as they join the cause for equality for all. I think about young people terrified of being bullied or outed and about adults who have struggled a lifetime with their identity. After reading the e-mails, I felt it to be only fair that I responded in an equally open and frank manner. Through sharing my battles with self-loathing, humiliation, and alcoholism, I hope others will gain the fortitude to live their lives openly with dignity, integrity and pride. For the Fred Phelps of the world, I hope our common humanity shows through to engender tolerance, if not acceptance.

My dad owned and operated a hardware store a couple of blocks from the large comfortable home in which I was raised. Each of my four siblings took our turn working in the store. I looked forward to it. I liked working, I liked interacting with customers, and I liked being with my dad. My parents, Bill and Mary Ann McCoy, were devout Catholics who saw to it their children attended mass every Sunday. They were also liberal Democrats devoted to raising strong independent children. I was a happy kid.

I would never have predicted how my life would unfold. As a child, I knew that something was different about me. I had feelings that differed from other kids in my class. I didn't understand my attraction to guys.

I lacked the hand-eye coordination of a lot of kids and because of this athletics involving a ball were not my thing. These were the sports that have always been strongly identified with the image of what it meant to be masculine. To be a real guy.

From an early stage, say from third grade on, I can recall being attracted to both men and women, but preferably men. This was something I dealt with by suppressing it. Throughout my parochial Catholic school education, I attended mass on almost a daily basis. I would fervently pray that this issue of liking boys would be resolved for me, that I wasn't different, and that I liked girls. Tortured prayers that poured out my distress to God went unanswered. They didn't work, at least as I had prayed. My confessions were in vain. Priests merely suggested I pray more and change my thoughts and behavior.

I remember at certain points through junior and senior high school I believed I actually was cured. But, I remember admitting to myself, "No, you're gay." Just the thought of possibly being gay was a hard thing to come accept. It was frightening. If my classmates knew about me, I would be made fun of, shamed, and shunned. It was a lonely feeling.

Although I had very loving and supportive parents, I did not feel in any way I could broach the subject with them. Nor did I dare breathe a word of it to anyone else involved in my Catholic education. I became imprisoned by my feelings and thoughts. Had I talked to my teachers and counselor they wouldn't have known what to do with me. They would have freaked out, sent me to confession, and reported me to my parents. I could do without the additional penance and guilt that would have been dumped on me. The subject of being gay was very, very taboo. It continued to painfully haunt me. I was always on guard fearing someone would find out. And boy did that take energy.

As I transitioned into high school, I had what I thought was a wonderful discovery that allowed me to become more comfortable in my own skin. The remedy I discovered was alcohol. Dowling Catholic High School was a parochial college prep school in Des Moines where the abundance and availability of alcohol was unlimited.

When I drank I became whoever I wanted to be without conscience or consideration for which I truly was. I believe this early use of alcohol contributed to my reliance and addiction that I later confronted as an adult. During my junior and senior years I drank almost daily. It seemed like everybody's parents were out of town on weekends, so there were a lot of house parties. Sometimes we had keggers in the country. Every weekend there was a party. I along with everyone else had fake IDs. Since the drinking age at the time was 19, fake IDs were easier to use by high school kids. We drank at kid's homes, in cars, and at parks after school.

I often drank to get drunk. Alcohol became my friend and an important part of anything I did from my junior year in high school through college. It allowed me to suppress my fears, guilt and pain so I could function. I was aware that alcohol made me feel better about myself, temporarily releasing me from those inner demons so why wouldn't I drink?

Prior to attending college, I began working for Vice President Walter Mondale on his presidential campaign. This was in 1984 and my first real exposure to politics. I served as high school student coordinator for the Mondale campaign. We volunteered and rallied for him. As part of our student government curriculum, students had to complete a dozen hours of volunteer work for a presidential campaign. All the metro high schools had this requirement. I coordinated other students. I spent a lot of hours bringing other students into the campaign and finding roles for them. We painted signs, door knocked, distributed bumper stickers on cars, made phone calls, and stuffed envelopes.

In June, 1987 Senator Joseph Biden began his campaign for president. I worked on his campaign my senior year in college. I really believed no one was smarter or more articulate than Joe Biden. He was charismatic. However, the following September Biden pulled out of the race following charges that he had plagiarized a speech.

I then began working for the Bruce Babbitt campaign in 1988. The work was exhilarating. He was hilarious. He actually rode RAGBRI which is a weeklong bike ride across Iowa. I found him to be a decent person who connected with average Iowans but lacked the money and organization to become a real force in presidential politics. In the meantime, I had found my niche.

In 1984 I entered Briar Cliff University, a Catholic university in Sioux City, Iowa. In college my passions and majors were American history and political science. I minored in speech. These studies prepared me well for what was to become my life's work.

Summers between college terms were spent working street construction throughout Des Moines, applying asphalt, tar, and seal coats. This work was enjoyable because it provided me an opportunity to feel my toughness as a very butch, macho guy who wanted everyone to believe that I was completely straight. After all, only manly men worked construction. Plus, the pay was pretty good.

It wasn't until college that I experimented with same-sex, sex with a student older than I. He was experienced. I was terrified. I was convinced I had contracted AIDS and immediately went to student health for a check-up. Self-loathing and promises to never ever experiment again occupied my thinking for days.

———————

I was brought up *knowing* that marriage was between a man and a woman. That was obvious to everyone. The only married people I knew were men who were married to women. People *choosing* to be gay didn't marry, and I never heard it mentioned. I have since come to know that gays and lesbians are born that way. After all, who would choose this harder path?

I also knew from my life experience, in viewing my parents' marriage and having been married to a wonderful woman, the sanctity that most married people hold for their marriage vows. I understand why gay people want to get married because it is such a uniquely important life experience. It is a public pronouncement of love and commitment deeper than any other. Its importance to same-sex couples is identical to that of straight couples. It also carries with it strong personal and legal prerogatives.

I also know from having been a Roman Catholic that God intended marriage to be only between a man and a woman. That was an absolute. Period. End of discussion. Well, only the end of the discussion for the Catholic Church. For many of us it created years of guilt and self-loathing.

As an adult I stayed closeted for survival, to save my job, to continue as a state senator, to save my family from embarrassment and humiliation, and most of all to save my marriage. I struggled against recognizing who I was or what I felt. I was terrified that someone would find out I was gay and out me.

Nothing is without its challenges. I avoided people and situations where someone might hurl a sexual slur or call to question my sexual orientation. I had no exposure as to what it meant to be gay let alone that there existed a flourishing underground gay community. Gay bars, cruising areas, after hour gatherings, parks, bookstores, and gay organizations were totally foreign to me. Even if I had known about them, I would have been too anxious to go near them. Today the internet gives uncensored exposure introducing this world to both gays and their straight counter-parts.

At age 26 I married after having convinced myself that I was simply bi-sexual and that those feelings of being attracted to men would pass. I certainly would not act upon them. Prior to marrying the woman whom I truly loved, we "played house" for nine months. I was happy. My wife was happy. We were happy. I knew I was cured. Looking back, I think my wife — with whom I have remained very close — wasn't the only one deceived in our marriage.

I met Jennifer (Jenny) Ann Stitt when I was 24 and she 23. A mutual friend introduced us at a bar and we began dating. She is a wonderful person — bright, hard working, happy, cheerful, optimistic and attractive. She was all the good things that I could ask for in a wife. Jenny is director of marketing for the book publishing group at Meredith Publishing.

Jenny and I were both interested in politics. However, at the time, she was more of a Republican with me being a strong liberal Democrat. We had great conversations. She was smart and articulate. We had fun. Jenny is genuine and to this day continues to be a great friend. She's somebody I completely trust.

I was in love with this wonderful gal who loved me in return. I loved her both romantically and as a friend. I sincerely believed that she and our marriage were the answer to my prayers. Our marriage wasn't a sham, a cover to protect my political career or me personally. I honestly felt our love would override any urges I had toward men. No longer did I have to deal with being gay.

We had a large wedding on May 29, 1993 at St Ambrose Cathedral in downtown Des Moines. Jenny put a lot of herself into the wedding, planning and doing the work that was involved in it. We focused on the ceremony and the commitment we were making. A children's choir sang. They were beautiful kids with beautiful voices. A symphony played. It was a magnificent time to get to know Jenny's family and for her family to get to know mine. Life was good. Life was going to continue to be good. Ours was a wedding to create lasting memories along with a lasting marriage. Well, ours lasted ten years.

Our son Jack McCoy was born May 13, 1999. We had waited six years for him, primarily because we were both busy getting careers established. In addition, Jenny was obtaining her Masters of Business Administration at Drake University. Our marriage was solid. We were in love, having fun with a lot in common.

But, about seven years into our marriage things began to change. One cost of having fast-paced lives where both husband and wife are heavily involved in many areas is that you risk living separate lives. We grew further and further apart. As our marriage began to fall apart, tension replaced love and laughter. I slid into alcoholism. We stopped living together as man and wife. I moved into separate housing — an unexpected blessing created by the redistricting of my senatorial district requiring me to either resign from my seat in the Senate or move. I moved and began my new life.

I continued to seek refuge in alcohol. This resolved nothing but my becoming an alcoholic. I was able to hide my alcoholism from my colleagues and the public. My life spiraled downward. During these stressful, painful days of my trying to understand what it meant to be gay, I sought out other divorced gay men to hear their stories. I wanted to learn how they dealt with becoming aware of their sexual orientation, their marriages, and their inevitable divorces. A pattern emerged of their not understanding the meaning of their attraction to men, of truly having been in love with their former wives, and of being in deep denial of being bi or gay. Self-loathing was common. Some thought they could "screw their way into being hetero." Didn't work for them. Didn't work for me. No one blamed their former spouse for their failed marriages. All regretted the agony they had put their wives through. I gained an insight into my life through these conversations. Their life patterns reflected my own life.

During the grueling years of my drinking, I found my behavior becoming more and more erratic. Certainly, sober, I would never have done some of the actions in which I now found myself. I began exploring my sexual orientation through a series of high risk behaviors which frankly always left me feeling empty and unsatisfied. This was just the opposite of what I wanted to achieve.

I tried a dozen times on my own to stop drinking. I failed each time and seemed to go deeper into the disease after each attempt failed. It became obvious, even to a drunk, that I needed help. I could not survive ending a marriage which had produced a child, overwhelming feelings of guilt, coming to grips with my sexual orientation, and combating alcoholism on my own. I finally obtained professional support. I attended Mercy Franklin outpatient treatment for alcoholism. It became clear that I had to first deal with my sexual orientation before coming to grips with my alcoholism.

Coming out to your wife is pure hell without having it played out in the press. As an elected official in my community, I had the unique role of having to come out in both my private and public life. I tried to face it with a degree of courage and honesty. Believe me, it required a lot of grit to overcome that anguish and humiliation to say nothing about the potential hurt I had inflicted on love ones.

When I chose public life I did not get to decide what I wanted to share or not share with the public. I had no choice; there are no secrets in Des Moines. I shared it all. Family became casualties because I had chosen public life. They were part of the shared spotlight. It is what it is. It would have been easier to just step down from public life and yell, "I want my private life. I don't want to be exposed to this scrutiny and I sure as hell don't want to drag my family through it." However, as an elected official with a decent sense of ethics, it was more honorable to stay involved and deal with my life as it came to me. This meant sharing my life experiences — the good, the bad and the ugly. Once I realized this and accepted it, I could actually get on with doing the job I was elected to do. That's what I did.

Coming out was liberating. For those people secure in their own sexuality this was not an issue. For the ignorant ones unsure in their sexuality, it was an issue.

———————

Until 1973, the American Psychiatric Association classified homosexuality as a mental illness which many thought could be cured. From this misconception, many jumped to the conclusion that to be gay was a choice. Numerous religious groups, along with self-righteous bigots, continue to declare this erroneous premise. That gays and lesbians are born that way is now backed by legitimate medical research.

People sometimes view others different from themselves as "abnormal." They, of course, are "normal." This standard creates broad criteria for what is commonly accepted as "normal." Putting others down reflects a sense of insecurity but apparently creates a sense of superiority for them. This is just plain wrong.

As a state senator, I have the dubious honor of being Iowa's highest ranking *openly* gay elected official. I once lived in constant fear of being outed. Now, I proclaim my sexuality with pride. Being out and open has enabled me to be honest with my family, my friends, my constituents, and equally important, myself. It has enabled me to openly advocate for acceptance and tolerance of the gay community, especially young people. Because I am on the public radar, I hope it has empowered people of all ages to realize life is good — even after coming out.

The e-mails in this book regarding marriage equality have synergy. My constituents and the people in my state have written me to share their experiences and opinions, good and bad, positive and negative. The stories and statements are raw with brutal honesty. I have a great deal of respect for all of them regardless of the position taken. They wrote me about how their opinions were formed and what marriage equality meant to them personally and spiritually. The e-mails are enlightening. Their stories expanded my understanding and resolve to use my position and influence to make a difference in their lives. I had become the point person in the legislature in the battle for marriage equality. I gladly accepted that position of leadership enabling me to make a difference, to make a huge paradigm shift, and to change our culture.

———————

I have grouped e-mails into chapters by themes. An overview opens each chapter. My comments, which were not necessarily sent to the writer, precede or follow many of the e-mails. E-mails had to be shortened and edited for publication. The privacy of the writers has been respected.

During the period leading up to the Supreme Court's decision on marriage equality, all legislators received hundreds of letters and e-mails urging them to take a specific stand. There were some letters via US mail but in general, the public has moved to e-mailing which is immediate, convenient and cheaper. There was an abundance of form letters sent on both sides of the issue. Bloggers were more direct in their language and opinions which they readily shared with the world under the cloak of anonymity.

Today, e-mails make up most of the correspondence received by legislators. They are written in a very informal style. Very few correspondences are addressed formally. The almost Victorian "Honorable Senator McCoy" is rarely used. When seen, it is most often from school kids.

Form letters are an efficient means to reach all legislators. In the same manner of efficiency, elected representatives often create response statements for specific topics. The efficiency of this for replying to dozens of e-mails on the same topic is obvious, plus everyone receives the same information on a given issue.

There were also a vast number of phone messages received on marriage equality. These were usually short and to the point. I'm not certain if this was due to callers being succinct or the receptionist summarizing messages. At any time, going through a stack of telephone messages provided insight on what was of current concern.

I read all correspondence. Those found in this book were over-whelming. Feelings of hope, inspiration, goodwill, or of anxiety, anger and hostility were all laid out. I put aside a pile of these to reflect on the mammoth impact this Supreme Court decision would make. I realized this correspondence constituted a narrative of the historical ruling about to take place. These e-mails are original artifacts — the stuff on which historians base their writings and opinions. History is made up of stories told by those involved. I felt these views and stories needed to be made public to put a human face on this historic civil rights movement.

I hope through these deeply personal stories and statements a greater understanding and respect will be achieved for all views expressed. I hope you will find them inspiring. These poignant views reflect values, cultures, life experiences, indoctrinations, and faith beliefs. We all cling to what we believe. We all want to believe we are "right" and "they" are wrong. Both sides of the issue are charged with emotion. However, rational thought is possible and it can still prevail.

Each of us has our own story, our personal history, and our own views emanating from our journey. Every voice is important. These e-mails combine to give us a macro view of this exciting time.

Chapter 2: No Longer Second Class Citizens

"As a same-gender couple, our six children and six grandchildren need to know their family is not second rate." (E-mail to Senator McCoy)

"The catastrophe of AIDS also help to inspire the quest for gay marriage. So much illness and death underscored agonizing inequalities: Lovers lacked the right to visit each other in hospitals or to oversee funeral arrangements."
(*The New Yorker*, November 12, 2012, Alex Ross p. 48)

I have listened to and read the stories of gay men as they looked back at their adolescent years. Emotional stories detailed individuals struggling with their sexual orientation. Stories related the enormous pressure felt to conform to societal expectations. These stories had much in common. They began with awareness that they were different but did not always understand why or even how. The barbs slung at them by peers stung — hurting deeply with potential permanent psychic damage. For survival, the young men built protective psychological walls of defense. They lived in constant fear that someone might out them or call them "queer." This became a way of life for young men struggling with their sexual identity. The religious guys, and not so religious ones, prayed to God to change them; to make them more masculine; and to forgive their sinful thoughts and shameful behavior. Anger, denial and self-loathing were prevalent. Sometimes the bullying, taunting, feelings of guilt and self-hatred became more then they could handle, culminating in death wishes. Tragically, for some young people their burdens ended in suicide.

Parental acceptance of who their child really is can provide the critical scaffolding needed during these developing years. Parental acceptance can make all the difference it the world. At least it will be one less cross their child has to bear. As some parents have shared, "I'd rather have a gay son than a dead one."

Ricky Martin, Latino pop singer sensation, came out on March 29, 2010 saying he was blessed for who he is. He later said if he had known how good it felt to be out in the open he would have done it years ago. As part of the coping transition process, he wrote his bestselling autobiography *ME* relating his years of denial, fear of being outed, and personal anguish. He packed his life with non-stop work to escape reflecting on his life and who he really was. Martin's sexual orientation had been widely questioned. He remained in the closet for fear that being openly gay would tank his career. Martin experienced the denial and fear of exposure experienced by many young people dealing with their sexual orientation. He expresses these feelings in the following excerpt:

> "We still have a long way to go. If the world has changed, I believe it still hasn't changed enough...There is a long and sad history of the persecution of homosexuals, and it is tragic to think about all the lives that have been damaged, hurt, and destroyed by the prejudices of others...Sadly, these prejudices continue to exist to this day...The very language used all over the world to denominate homosexuals is terribly degrading: words such as 'faggot,' 'queer,' 'dyke,' 'sissy,' and others, which only serve to perpetuate hatred and discrimination among the younger generations. Because of the emotional charge they carry, such words quietly create an atmosphere of intolerance and homophobia, in which young people are afraid to be what they really are..."

"Battling Prejudice" from Ricky Martin's autobiography *ME* (Celebra, Published by New American Library, a division of Penguin Group [USA], New York, New York, 2010, pages 260-261.)

Some parents have told me they knew their child was gay before their coming out and in some cases knew their child was gay before their child did.

Struggles didn't cease with adulthood. Grown people related their agonizing journey in establishing a legal relationship with their partner. A plea for the security that recognized same-gender marriage would bring was often expressed.

As an outspoken Senator in support of marriage equality, the number of positive e-mails I received outnumbered the negative. People from all over the state and nation seemed to sense the need to have my back as they encouraged me to continue our battle for equal rights.

McCoy: E-mails from university professors.

"Too much time has been wasted on fruitless discussions about constitutional amendments banning same-sex marriage. According to The Iowa Constitution this would be abhorrent. It would effectively legalize discrimination against countless families and individuals in this state. This is un-American and certainly counter to the values of Iowa. The beliefs of conservative religious zealots about gay and lesbian families, while deeply felt, are not relevant on this issue. The ruling of the Iowa Supreme Court very clearly protects their religious beliefs and the rights of churches to define religious marriage in whatever way they wish. But it also, very elegantly, provides appropriate rights and protections to gays and lesbians in Iowa. The rights of citizenship ARE NOT dependent on religious approval in a country that believes in the separation of church and state. The rights of Iowa citizens CANNOT BE DEPENDENT on whether or not other citizens disapprove of our lives and identities. We have a governmental system of checks and balances in order to ensure that discriminatory public opinion does not succeed in ruling the day. The court's ruling overturning the ban on same-sex marriage may not be popular with everyone, but it is RIGHT."

McCoy: Another professor wrote:

"As a professor of ethics, I would also like to add that there is NO ethical justification that justifies preventing gay and lesbian couples from marrying. I will be embarrassed and disgusted if Iowa does not protect the rights of everyone."

———

McCoy: Writers viewed firsthand the struggle same-sex couples go through to access benefits entitled to spousal couples.

"Allowing couples of the same sex to marry isn't going to kill anyone. Same-sex marriage is not just about the love and commitment these people want to make to each other. As someone who works in the insurance world, same sex couples face the struggles of not being able to have the same spousal benefits on investments such as annuities or life insurance like any other 'couple' would have. Same-sex couples having to leave money to your 'friend' instead of your spouse results in these funds being taxed differently on the state and federal levels. Even in death a person's wishes can be overridden by blood family relatives, disregarding the wishes of the surviving partner. This can range from decisions related to burial rites, cremation or burial location."

———

McCoy: A compassionate writer shared her anguish of having watched her brother struggle with coming to terms with his sexual identity.

My brother, who is gay, lives in Seattle and was so proud that Iowa is one of only three states to allow committed couples to marry regardless of what they look like. Anyone who thinks a person has a choice in their sexual identity is either naïve or living under a rock. I watched my brother struggle with his sexual identity and it is not a choice. It is who he is. Why should people be punished for being who God made them? Tolerance is a Christian virtue, hate is not. Why are these people worried? Are they fearful gay couples will have a lower divorce rate than heterosexual couples?"

McCoy: An e-mailer from Canada reminded us the concern about equality is world-wide.

"Your state has made itself a beacon of inclusiveness throughout the United States with its recent decision to support equal marriage. You must be exceptionally proud, as are we in Canada who fought for full equal marriage. Your own story is inspiring for future generations of LGBT kids."

McCoy: A writer from my past contacted me.

"I live in your district and used to work with you years ago at Younkers Department Store. I know you support freedom to marry and I urge you to continue to fight the extreme right wing people who don't understand why the right for all people to marry will not affect them (forget about trying to explain to them it is a basic human right - they don't want to hear that). Churches are still able to refuse to marry anyone (including heterosexual couples).

McCoy: Writers covered a broad range of topics.

"Matt CONGRATULATIONS…A RED LETTER DAY INDEED!!!!"

"Let's lead the nation by example and show them that Iowans will not tolerate discrimination of any kind and that all Iowans will be treated equally."

"Kids suffer in divorces. Marriage is not limited only to whether to have sex or to bear children. It is about commitment, trust and responsibility. Either type of marriage can be abusive, cheating, horrible. I strongly believe that people should be in charge of their own lives and happiness. Society needs to stop intruding into their bedrooms. All of us would like to grow old with whomever we please."

―――――――

"I have been with my partner for almost 20 years. This law means everything to me. We have always proudly exercised our right to love who we choose. Our families and our friends came to see us marry in our church in 1995. It is time that our leaders and politicians get behind us, too. I believe marriage equality will not have any effect on anyone else's life other than to enrich and improve their lives by allowing us to be visible and recognized as who we are."

―――――――

"To do otherwise than support the constitutional right to marry is to pander to the less noble aspects of humanity that will diminish all of us."

―――――――

"I have been with my partner for 13 years and we are thrilled to be able to make it official."

―――――――

"Please give Senator McCoy a high five from me."

―――――――

"It is never the right thing to do to take away other people's civil liberties and equal rights."

―――――――

"You can't vote away love."

"I just wanted to commend your strength and courage in standing firm against those who would want to amend OUR constitution to read that only a select population is entitled to equal protection under the laws of Iowa. I'm profoundly aware that, if not for people like you who have the courage to stand up for the rights of others, my life would look tragically different."

"I am a proud lesbian, and have been with my partner for almost 20 years. We have raised three children; one who died at the age of 21 and the other two are productive citizens who still live in Iowa. I just want that freedom to marry the woman I fell in love with, and still love after 20 years."

"I realize gay marriage is a hot button topic for many people. We've got a lot of problems with the economy, health care, education, etc. Please focus on these core items."

"My two year old nephew was nearly as excited as his uncles, who have been together for 17 years, and were now able to be married. I imagine that in 20 years I will tell him how his uncles were once not allowed to be married and how he will look at me in disbelief. This is the same way that most of us today have a hard time imagining that my nephew's mom and dad, an interracial couple, would not have had access to legal marriage just a short time ago. And to think it happened in Iowa."

"Our openly gay son is a Des Moines Roosevelt High School graduate and National Merit Scholar. He currently lives and works in Chicago. Please help ensure that some of our brightest may feel welcome to come home to a state that has recognized that none can be discriminated against."

"Hearing our legislative leaders speak out on behalf of justice at the downtown rally following the decision of the Supreme Court, I have to tell you as a heterosexual, married person, I felt *safe*. Hearing the supportive reactions of my friends and family from around the country has been amazing. Hearing my dad say how happy he was about the ruling (when he would have opposed this even 3-4 years ago) is even more amazing. Like you, I've devoted my life to public service. Thanks for everything you're doing."

"Add my name to the list of fair-minded Iowans who support equality in Iowa. I'm doing my best to help all of my friends, neighbors, co-workers and others understand that I deserve the same rights as they do."

"As a person of goodwill, I believe in marriage equality for all people."

"The Iowa Supreme Court has spoken. That's sufficient."

McCoy: If only that was true. Cases throughout the country will be pushed up to the U.S. Supreme Court for their rulings that will impact the entire country. I can't wait until that happens.

"Iowa is now on the forefront of marriage equality and will be an inspiration for other states to follow."

"As a registered Republican I probably did not vote for you. However, I want to let you know that even though I am not gay, I strongly support the recent decision from the Iowa Supreme Court and I encourage you to oppose any attempts to ban same-sex marriage. In the next election I plan to vote against any Republican who makes gay marriage an issue, assuming their opponent doesn't do the same."

McCoy: You are exactly on the right track. You have changed your perspective. Sean Strub notes in *Body Count*, "No amount of social activism will change the world until enough of us change ourselves." (*Body Counts: A Memoir of Politics, AIDS, and Survival*, by Sean Strub, Scribner, A Division of Simon & Schuster, Inc., NY, NY @ 2014)

"My partner and I are both physicians. We have been together 16 years and would like to get married. We think there are more pressing matters for our government to be addressing at this time and hate to see precious time used on this issue."

"Please resist the now resounding cry of havoc and the desire of some to unleash the dogs of war to protect Iowa and America from judicial activism, communist conspiracies and all manner of dire results emanating from the Supreme Court's ruling. Denying rights and freedoms to a particular class of individuals smacks mightily of Germany as the Weimar Republic was collapsing and Nazism was rising."

"We need to be courageous – to fight for equal rights."

McCoy: You are correct in saying "to fight for equal rights." *The Des Moines Sunday Register* (February 23, 2014, p. 6A) reported the Iowa Civil Rights Commission had 87 discrimination complaints in 2013 based on sexual orientation. Please continue your campaign for justice.

"Now, after seven wonderful years, my partner and I can be legally recognized by the state of Iowa. I had accepted the fact that I would never be able to have a true wedding, exchange rings with the one I loved nor be able to have the same respect and rights as married couples. Without the dedication and assistance that you have given, this day may not have been possible and my dream may have never come true. I ask that you continue to stand behind the rights of all human-kind and against any attempts at a constitutional amendment."

"As a Drake student and as a transsexual, seeing that I can marry the person I love no matter what my birth certificate says is a wonderful feeling. I want to thank you for your determined stance and tireless effort to further the rights of the LGBT community."

"As a medical student ready to leave the state for rotations, this court decision has proven to me that Iowa is a state worth returning to and raising my children."

"I have been in a committed relationship for 17 years and raised two children who are now college graduates. All families need to feel supported and equal. Please do not amend the Constitution to go backward."

"I am a medical student at Des Moines University. The Supreme Court stood up for equal rights, no matter what a person's differences. Do not let the decision be reversed as it will negatively reflect on the state's history and future. All people deserve to be treated as equals, not just those who are judged to be considered so."

"Hello from Savannah, Georgia! Way to go Iowa Supreme Court. I have had dozens of people mention this great event. People were buzzing and saying 'As Iowa goes, so goes the nation.'" (Georgia)

——— ———

"Please stick to your decision. LGBT citizens are not second class citizens, we should have all the same rights as heterosexuals."

——— ———

"As a heterosexual I appreciate this decision as it upholds the civil rights of all citizens and blocks interference from those who want to take them away."

——— ———

"I urge you to stay strong, since ultraconservative groups are surely flooding your office with vitriolic phone calls and e-mails. Your courage in the face of right-wing pressure has helped ensure that no loving, committed couple is denied the protections of marriage."

——— ———

"I know you are facing immense pressure right now about same-sex marriage. My husband and I are proud to be a part of a state that honors equal protection for everyone. It is a chance for us to be brave pioneers in the face of ignorance and hatred."

——— ———

"Just because it isn't everyone's cup of tea doesn't mean that a certain group of people should be denied their basic human rights."

——— ———

"Our state motto is 'Our Liberties We Prize and Our Rights We Will Maintain.' A state this committed to freedom and individual rights should not have bigotry enshrined in its constitution."

——— ———

"I have been with my partner for seven years now. We have a house in the Drake University neighborhood, have paid our taxes, and have done everything asked of us to make the area better. We have voted in the school board elections, voted for the new Polk County Jail and have served our community! We deserve to be treated equally! We have earned it! Please don't amend the Constitution!!"

——— ———

"My wife and I are hard-working Iowans, and love living in Iowa. We have two great daughters, ages 28 and 25. We raised them in a loving Christian home. We love them both a lot. They are both responsible, hard-working young adults. One is gay, one is straight.

The gay daughter realized she was not heterosexual at age 20. She now has had a wonderful young woman as a partner/roommate/best friend for five years. They would like to get married. We would like to see that commitment too, and we want that happiness for them. It's not their fault they are gay. It's not my fault. It's not your fault. It's nobody's fault. They just are!

Please don't encourage Iowa laws designed to prevent them from getting married or designed to exclude them from the same rights as other U.S. citizens. It's none of your business. It doesn't affect you. It affects ME and my daughter and her right to happiness. What if it was YOUR daughter?"

——— ———

"I find myself flabbergasted that there are people who want to use precious government resources to perpetuate hate."

——— ———

"KEEP GAY MARRIAGE LEGAL! I am a white man married to a black women. We love each other and are committed to spending the rest of our lives together. But a little over 40 years ago, our marriage would have been illegal in much of the United States. Many would have seen our marriage as unnatural, disgusting, and immoral — the same bigoted terms being thrown about to describe gay marriage today.

If I weren't married to my wife, I would have to go through life describing her simply as my 'girlfriend,' or worse, pretending that we're just good 'friends.' Neither of those words describes the relationship we have. We are husband and wife. We are family. And it means a lot to us that the laws don't discriminate against us.

No one today would advocate a vote on whether my wife and I could be married. Letting others vote on our rights would be seen as cruel and absurd. I suggest that letting the public vote on anyone's rights is just as cruel and absurd. People who are committed to being a family with one another deserve to be married, regardless of their sex, race, or religion. The people at certain times would not have voted against slavery, or against denying women suffrage, or against my own marriage. Rights for those without power are too valuable to let the majority decide on them."

McCoy: I was asked by somebody who was in Iowa doing an article for *Time Magazine*, "What makes Iowa different from California? Why do you think Iowa is going to go along with this when California did not?" Excellent question. I replied, "For one thing, Iowans are better educated. Iowans have a sense of fairness. That means trusting people equally not only in the work place but in finding a way for other people to fulfill their dreams and hopes."

"What a joy it was to me to hear of the favorable ruling for same sex-marriage by the Iowa Supreme Court. Around 1975, I

took our first gay delegation to meet with Iowa Governor Robert
Ray. At the time I was the pastor of the fledging Des Moines
Metropolitan Community Church, a gay community seeking to
worship together. We were to talk to Governor Ray about
dropping the sodomy laws from the criminal codes as the
legislature was in the process of revising the codes. Lt. Gov. Neu
met with us as Governor Ray was in Russia with a trade
delegation. Lt. Gov. Neu assured us the sodomy laws would be
dropped from the books and they were.

I was especially concerned as I had a parishioner who had
been sentenced to ten years in the Iowa prisons under the law. He
and another man were caught in a washroom at Sears. The other
man was put on probation because he was not the aggressor and
my parishioner got 20 years because he was caught sucking the
man off. At the time my parishioner was a church organist. So, in
34 years Iowa has come a long ways." (Sacramento, CA)

"The people of Iowa have no business voting on this. When
the Iowa Supreme Court ruled back in the 19th Century that a
slave was a free person here on Iowa soil, that did not go to a
vote. What would have happened had people in some parts of the
U.S. been allowed to vote on interracial marriage in the 1950s?
No democracy worth its salt allows a majority to vote on the
rights of a minority. Those Democrats with a backbone need to
be educating the people of Iowa regarding this."

"I would like to thank you for the inspirational words that
you delivered regarding the Iowa Supreme Court's decision to
legalize gay marriage. I am a young gay man, Iraq War Veteran
and will be graduating from law school in May. I was humbled
by your words supporting the Court's decision. I hope to one day
visit your wonderful state. It is people like you who help not only
gays and lesbians, but other minorities secure their rights in the
courts."

"Will our civilization end because of the recent Iowa Supreme Court decision allowing gay marriage? There are a lot of fundamentalists who seem to think so. Have you read Gibbon's <u>Decline and Fall of the Roman Empire</u>? According to him, it was Christianity that brought the Empire down! How? Orthodoxy was the culprit. The newly created Christians, in their enthusiasm, decided they were too good to cooperate with pagans or with heretical Christians who did not believe in the divinity of Christ. The Empire fell, not because of sex, orgies or immorality, it was economics and a weakened military state due to rejection, for religious reasons, of former allies. So, I don't think the current court decision will result in the permanent decline and destruction of civilization. Christian conservatives need to see the big picture and have sympathy for all of God's children, not just those like them!"

"You have given the community a reason to believe in government that protects the people instead of being subjected to tyrannical mob rule. That is the essence of true democracy."

McCoy: "When the Iowa Supreme Court ruled on Friday that gays can marry in the Hawkeye State, gay marriage became not just a coastal thing. Deep in the rural heartland, a straightforward opinion —written by a justice appointed by a conservative Republican governor — methodically eviscerates one argument after another that for decades has been used to keep marriage the sole preserve of straight couples. 'This class of people asks a simple and direct question: How can a state premised on the constitutional principle of equal protection justify exclusion of a class of Iowans from civil marriage?' Justice Mark S. Cady asked. The answer? It can't." (*Time Magazine*, Michael A. Lindenberger, Saturday, April 04, 2009.)

"I was sitting in the airport waiting for my flight when I heard the news. I was suddenly overjoyed that the years of work and efforts seemed to have finally paid off. I was thinking that I can get married now, and honestly, I would not be able to use the law as an excuse to avoid a commitment to someone special. In that moment, I felt an instant closer connection to my love than ever before (despite the miles between us at that moment). On that quiet day in April, in Iowa, couples finally did not have to pretend that they were married or think that their relationship was always less than the neighbor's. Finally, couples did not have to hide their relationships from the law, to feel inherently unequal, to feel inferior to others around them in loving relationships. Further, no 'tradition' or current marriage seemed to be on the edge of collapse or destruction because of the ruling.

Hopefully, people can lower the veils of hatred and narrow mindsets to allow all people to continue their personal, loving and legal relationships. While our relationships did not affect theirs, they should have the decency to not affect ours, and where we respect their intimate, private affairs as personal, so they should with us."

"There is not one argument used against this action that was not once used against slavery and Jim Crow. Modern science, medicine and psychiatry nearly universally say we are born as we are with various sexual orientations. Why would anyone want to be tormented, even killed, for choosing something that would cause you to be treated so horribly? Do you know how many suicides among youth are the results of torment and rejections for being gay? Some parents would rather have their child dead than gay. Religion that produces these results is really demonic.

Divorce threatens marriage. Child abuse, like that committed by my farm neighbor who raped his 15 year old daughter over a long period of continual sexual intercourse, destroys marriage. TV, movies, priests abusing boys, protestant clergy messing with females, prostitution, pornography can all threaten and/or destroy marriage. But show me one thing that gay marriage does to damage marriage. God excludes no one God has created. Friday was a great day in Iowa."

"Love finally conquered hate. Please let the hate roll off and uphold this decision."

"I am so proud of you and your state which is furthering its illustrious history for equal rights. Congratulations." (California)

"Iowa is beginning to be heard. The story about the Iowa Supreme Court's decision was featured on CNN tonight." (Colorado)

"We have been together for eight years and recently became engaged. Iowa is our home and we look forward to building a family here with the same rights as heterosexual couples."

"I have just watched your You Tube video about Iowa's new marriage rights for same-sex couples. I'm astonished and delighted and, frankly, I'm weeping with such mixed emotions: happiness, pride, hope, and a little envy! I sometimes feel as if Texas will never give my partner and me the equal status we long for, and the California reversal was such a devastating blow. We thought, 'if not California, then WHERE?' Now, I hope all states will follow your lead." (Texas)

"My partner and I are thrilled with the marriage ruling."

"Our heterosexual marriage is actually that of two bisexual people. As an interracial couple we are part of a brave history of advocacy for marriage equality. Just 50 years ago, it was illegal for a black person to marry a white person in many states. It took a Supreme Court decision in 1967 (Loving vs. Virginia) to strike down those laws. We believe that denying rights to one group based on some immutable personal quality, such as the race or sex, is unjust and ultimately immoral. We believe that marriage should be accessible to all couples willing to make this tremendous commitment, regardless of the sex of the partners. Just as brave interracial couples and their allies dared to challenge the racist system that limited access to marriage for some couples; we join our voices with same-sex couples and other allies to challenge the homophobic and heterosexist system that denies marriage equality to all. The system must change! We offer our story as a reminder that things can change and as another call for justice and equality for all Iowa families."

———— ⋄ ————

"I find myself writing to you as the father of a gay teenage son. My son is home schooled. Being gay and a teen in Iowa is often times a difficult thing. When people say to him that being gay is a chosen life style, he responds, 'Why would anyone choose to be gay?' As you receive pressure from anti-gay and lesbian groups who will tell you they are speaking on behalf of your constituents, I ask you to ask yourself what actions would I be taking if my son or daughter were gay or lesbian? What actions would I take if the person I loved more than words can describe told you this? Like me you would do what is best for this person for whom you cared. You would do all in your power to help to make a good life for them."

———— ⋄ ————

"We are a same sex-couple who have been committed to each other since 1984. My former wife supports us as do our children. We all celebrate holidays together. Society must get with the 21st Century. There are many kinds of families. We deserve the right to be legally married!"

———————

McCoy: There is pain in growing up gay. A loving, accepting family can make a difference.

"My parents disowned me as a result of my coming out. I cannot believe that I will not be allowed to marry the man I will someday find and love. I will marry, not to spite my parents, but in spite of them."

———————

"As a 37 year old gay man in a committed relationship, this ruling is vitally important to me, my partner, and our family. We were one of the 26 same-sex couples who received marriage licenses back in August 2007. Even though a stay was executed on Judge Hanson's ruling at the time, my partner and I moved forward with our plans and were formally married on May 24, 2008. All of our friends, family members, co-workers, and acquaintances recognize us as a married couple. With last Friday's Iowa Supreme Court ruling, we finally have the legal backing of the state to protect our marriage and the legal right to take care of one another in times of need and receive the same benefits that are automatically granted to a select few at birth."

———————

"As a 70 year old with the benefit of a 27 year relationship with a wonderful man, I see great advantages in marriage equality. We have seen this same evolution of equality positively impact women, Jewish people, African-Americans, those with handicaps, and other identifiable groups associated with negative attitudes and stereotypes. I am retired now. I was 'out' at work. That was only possible because of specific language in personnel policies that provided the needed protections."

———————

McCoy: Iowa families who have a connection with gay people need to tell their stories. Stories about the love you feel for your partner and the love you feel for your children touch people. Sharing with people that we have the same dreams for our lives, for our children as everyone else will build common ground. That's really all we're asking people to do is to realize that we are all the same. These stories will sustain our movement, change hearts and minds that will lead to action. To do nothing is to support those groups actively opposing marriage equality.

"African Americans were enslaved in this country for over 200 years, beaten, murdered, and degraded beyond imagination. It was legal and constitutional. They had to fight long and hard for even the smallest bit of protection under the law. The fight is not over but as a state and nation we should be able to see that it was never right, never moral, never truer. We cannot go backwards by trying to pass laws that take away any person's civil rights or that allow for legal discrimination."

"I am not a native Iowan but am really proud that I live in Iowa. I don't believe the people of Iowa should be allowed to vote on this issue. If the people of this country had been allowed to vote on the Civil Rights Bill, I believe we would still be a segregated society. Not because the majority of people wouldn't have chosen to support civil rights, but because the opposition would have been so loud, threatening, and menacing that people's resolve would have wilted with the onslaught. I'm afraid the same could happen with this issue in Iowa as it did in California."

"I just read your statement on Iowa's State Supreme Court decision on *Daily Kos*. From one Eagle Scout to another — Kudos, sir." (California)

McCoy: It was especially reinforcing to receive endorsement from pastors throughout Iowa.

"May I take just a moment to express a word of thanks to you for your excellent YouTube video regarding the Iowa Supreme Court ruling? And thanks as well for your work on behalf of gay rights in Iowa. We are all being blessed through the efforts, courage, and decency of you and the many who have worked to make marriage equality a dream-come-true in this great state. Again, thank you!" (Pastor)

McCoy: An inmate at a nearby correctional facility shared his views on marriage equality. His handwritten letter was sent to me at the State House through the U.S. Postal Service.

"Honorable Matt McCoy: I am an inmate at Newton Correctional Facility. I learned about the proceedings over the gay marriage rights. I am not gay but it is my belief that in the United States of American people are able to choose what they want. No one should be able to tell another who they can or cannot love. I have friends that are gay and I would say without a doubt that they are more loyal as friends than the straight friends I have. I have never had one of them stab me in the back like even my own family has done to me. Please let this letter stand as my statement that gays have rights and should be treated just like anyone else. I am a Christian and I do believe in the Bible but, I also have very strong beliefs that people should be able to choose their life."

"Hold strong against those who oppose our human rights." (Maryland)

McCoy: This adult still feels the pain of growing up "different," growing up gay in an intolerant world. Rural areas, with a small population of gays, often are without support. The intolerance (bullying) can be fierce, often leading to suicide.

"It isn't easy standing up for gay rights in Iowa. I know because I grew up in Sioux City, IA and went to Drake University back in the 70s and 80s when you didn't tell people you were a lesbian. I marched in my first gay pride parade in Des Moines and attended my first protests there. Iowa has come a long way! Iowans are good people, they are just stubborn and very resistant to change, but change is coming. I left Iowa years ago and moved to the west coast where I could feel safe, safe to have a life, find a partner and raise a child, but you are making my home state safe for the queer and straight youth to come. Don't get discouraged."

———————

"If Iowa goes backwards and again imposes discrimination against same sex couples' right to marry, it will not be surprising to see brilliant young couples quickly fleeing Iowa. Our son and his partner have been together for ten years with combined incomes of $200K. I have told them to leave Iowa if they are not given the right to marry."

———————

Chapter 3: Your Personal Views Are Not Relevant — LET US VOTE!

"Our journey is not complete until our gay brothers and sisters are treated like anyone else under the law, for if we are truly created equal, then surely the love we commit to one another must be equal, as well."

President Barack Obama
Inaugural Address, January 21, 2013

Threats, name-calling, scolding and being misinterpreted or intentionally misquoted all come with being a politician. Some of it is very personal, some absurd, some seems off the wall, and some of it actually hurts. It's meant to be personal, thus it's impossible not to be taken personally. It seems some writers take pride in their bigotry.

Iowa Senate Majority Leader Mike Gronstal refused to allow the question of same sex-marriage to come before the Senate. He also refused to allow a bill calling for a state constitutional convention to be presented. This created a firestorm. Opponents to same-gender marriage were furious and eager to share their feelings.

I read all correspondence, making a mental note to ascertain patterns. A real effort is made to respond to all e-mails and letters — some I even take-on. And, no, I don't lose votes I never had. My life experiences along with years in the public have thickened my skin for survival.

Opposing forces feed off each other, creating strong reactions from each side. They are not necessarily equal but their combined magnitude can activate masses of people sometimes verging on mob hysteria.

The beauty of a democracy is that we all have the freedom — the right — to present our views in a peaceful manner. Some of this is done through electing officials with similar views to our own. Some of it is through directly communicating with elected officials already in office. Those opposed to marriage equality were not shy in letting me know their positions. I totally got it. I understood. They spoke with an abundance of clarity.

Some e-mails reflected strong religious convictions, some were obviously programmed, while others truly sounded concerned for the welfare of our state, country, and yes, even our souls, particularly mine!

E-mails came from all over Iowa as well as from other states. Responding to correspondence from my constituents is a priority that I take seriously. I am grateful for all letters, as together they create a broad perspective of issues. E-mails from people not particularly pleased with me on marriage equality follow in this chapter.

———————

Matt: An e-mail from Florida:

"I am a born again Christian and I am totally against same-sex marriages. The Bible clearly teaches against the union of same-sex. If this is allowed to stand, I hate to see what God will do to the United States for its clearly denying God, and this abomination. I beg you to do whatever you can to strike these opinions down and keep our country safe." (Florida)

McCoy: You don't want to have gay marriage? Don't have one. My god is not a god of hate. How can people who love God preach hate? My god is accepting of all people created in his own likeness. Thus, how can being gay be against God's will when a person has no choice in how s/he has been created? You are born with your God-given sexuality. Remember, Christ identified with the persecuted.

———————

McCoy: Letters were sometimes short, to the point but leaving no doubt as to their position.

"LET US VOTE!"

"I know when we elect people to represent us and they don't do their jobs or what they say they believe in, then we as a freedom speech (sic) get to voice our thoughts. Equality is not gays sire, equality is black or Hispanic or a woman. They do not have a choice to be who they are. And I would love to know how to run for office, any advice would be greatly appreciated. Thank you for your time and your thoughts. You are one of only a few legislators who has responded to my e-mails."

McCoy: Check with our Secretary of State where you can secure forms necessary for gathering the required number of support signatures to enable your name to appear on the ballot. I recommend that you spend some time observing the political process by attending meetings and public hearings.

"Thank you sir again for your reply. We may not see eye-to-eye on things but I do respect you for taking a stand and your willingness to take your time to correspond with someone outside your district."

"We the people are your boss, and if you don't hear our voice and allow us to vote on the marriage amendment then you will be held accountable on Election Day."

"It is disappointing that the legislature is taking the stance that the court should be deciding the law rather than the people that elected them. Fortunately, we have the ability to change the elected officials. I now have a clear view of your stance on the issue."

"I would like you to protect traditional marriage in Iowa. Let the citizens of Iowa vote on this most important issue affecting the families of Iowa." (Oklahoma)

"Please give Iowan's the chance to vote on the Marriage Amendment." (Tennessee)

McCoy: Here's the thing, I will not vote for discrimination. Slaves could not legally marry. I see a parallel to those now opposed to marriage equality. For me to vote for a marriage amendment limiting marriage to between a man and a women would be voting the death penalty for civil rights.

"I am not a person who is easily outraged. Nor have I ever undertaken to write a state representative. This attempt, however, to initiate such reprehensible behavior as to amend or repeal existing law through inappropriate channels has driven me to action. Whatever problems we have in America must be addressed through 'due process.' The duty of a judge is to uphold the existing law. There must be serious consequence for stepping outside of the given sphere of responsibility. The legislative authority together with the minds and hearts of the American people is the proper arena to make such a monumental decision. I have done my part by making my voice heard. Please do your part and fight to protect the American system of justice." (Louisiana)

"You need to stop standing between Iowans and our right to vote on the Iowa Marriage Amendment. Let me remind you that you were hired to represent the people of our district, not a vocal minority who want to limit our right to vote. Regardless of your position personally you need to let us exercise our God given right to vote. What are you and others afraid of?"

McCoy: Somewhere I remember reading, "A government that rules by majority only cannot be just."

"It is now time for you, as our elected representative, to stand up to the Iowa Supreme Court and denounce their ruling as unconstitutional and further declare that anyone that violates Iowa law by issuing a marriage license to any couple other than 'one man and one woman' is in violation of Iowa law and will be punished as such. Please accept your responsibility in this matter and do what you were elected to do."

"A 'living' constitution is really no constitution at all. If the constitution means whatever we want it to, it is truly meaningless. The legislature is the branch of government to deal with and face the changing and actual world. If we personally want a world of unlimited baby killing and lap dancing on every corner we should look to legislatures to allow it, not the courts. Executive and legislative powers exercised by the judicial branch of government cannot possibly be constitutional.

What can YOU possibly do? Thank the courts for their opinion but express that it is one that is not recognized by the citizens of this state and they should spend more time following their duties rather than usurp the duties of legislatures. Remind them who controls their purse strings. As an alternative, resign."

McCoy: Iowa Courts are a separate and co-equal branch of government. The courts have acted within their authority and their decision stands.

"In a recent Hawkeye Poll, fewer than 30% of Iowa voters support same-sex marriage. In 31 out of 31 states where voters have had a chance to vote on marriage, they supported traditional marriage."

––––––––––

"Please do not allow the Iowa courts to usurp your authority and make a mockery of marriage. Marriage has been, is, and should always be the sacred union between one man and one woman." (Virginia)

McCoy: Our judicial system did the job it was created to do.

––––––––––

"Once again our state legislature seems to have waited until the end of the session when everyone wants to go home to push bills through that IOWANS don't want. Come on, certainly you and others can get something started so Iowans can begin the process to define marriage as between one man and one woman."

––––––––––

"It's strange that homosexuality has been around for centuries in this world and never has it been considered as a marriage environment situation. I know that you voted against the marriage amendment, which truly saddens me. As a registered independent, my vote will be up for grabs next election. I can guarantee that, as one of your constituents, I will be voting for your competition if you continue to oppose the marriage amendment."

McCoy: Throughout the State of Iowa and across the nation citizens have been celebrating the unanimous decision of the Iowa Supreme Court.

"Well, Matt, I'll be voting for your opposition in any campaign you run."

––––––––––

"I am happily married with three young children and am very upset about the Court's ruling. I am thinking about our state's future and what kind of people this will attract. I do not want to have to explain to my young children why two men or two women are kissing like *that* in public. It is outrageous to consider this as a tool to bring in more money for the state. Do we really want to give up our traditional values for the sake of extra tourism money? Do we want Iowa to become the Mecca for homosexuals this side of the Appalachian Mountains?"

McCoy: We don't all share the same rights, some are denied gays and other minorities. But, speaking of tourism money, One Iowa estimated $12-$13 million was spent by gay couples in Iowa during Iowa's first year of marriage equality.

"The decision by the Supreme Court is anti-family AND unconstitutional! Take your power back!"

McCoy: Anti-family? Actually, it is a victory *for families*. The Iowa House Judiciary Committee held a public hearing on January 31, 2011, on its proposed constitutional amendment to ban gay marriage. Zach Wahls, a 19-year-old sixth generation Iowan, was an engineering student at The University of Iowa. Wahls told his story about being raised by two moms who were in a long term relationship. His moms married once same gender marriage was legal in Iowa. The packed House listened in awe as Wahls told legislators that what made them a family was the love that bond them. The Eagle Scout's speech was riveting. Total silence followed. Then Wahls was given a thunderous standing ovation. His speech went viral on YouTube eventually having over 18 million hits.

McCoy: Courts do not create rights not found in the Constitution.

"You and the others that support the gay marriage rights are wrong. Using the argument that this is popular and therefore the right thing to do is the exact same argument that Hitler and Stalin used, and it led their countries and people to disastrous ends. This issue and decision carries with it the exact same ends for our culture and society. You may not see it now or maybe it will not even be evident for some time to come, but unleashing gay marriage will most certainly lead to disastrous results for our cities, our state, our country, our culture and our society at large. This is not a civil rights issue. It is not a fairness issue. It is not progress, but it does have an impact. The decision to support gay marriage is a foundational cultural change that will bring with it significant and maybe irreparable harm to the sanctity of holy matrimony between a man and a woman and to our society at large. The historical record on this is crystal clear. If we do not stand up against this effort to change the definition of marriage that has stood the test of time for centuries past, then we are destined to repeat the same mistakes that have brought down the greatest societies that have preceded ours, but were laid to ruin for the same reasons that we find before us right now. This will most certainly be the trumpet that brings the walls of our cities crashing down upon us."

McCoy: I am in agreement that this change in our laws is significant. I believe in an individual's right for happiness and in protecting an individual's civil rights to be treated equally. By denying civil rights to a minority you threaten the civil rights for the majority.

Ferguson: I was at a conference lunch sitting with several protestant ministers. In discussing marriage equality, the ministers agreed it would damage traditional marriages. I asked how it would cause damage to my 35-year secure marriage? One-by-one the ministers left the table without elaborating on how marriage equality would irreparably harm my marriage. Why didn't they provide evidence to support their assertions? Because there wasn't any.

"There is room for civil unions in a secular pluralist society (which we are), but I don't support the idea of either homosexual or plural marriage, or any other change to the traditional understanding of marriage."

McCoy: "Civil marriage involves a state license…Civil marriage law was historically used to legally encode segregation. Blacks and whites couldn't marry each other in some states until the Supreme Court overturned 'miscegenation' laws in 1967." (*Attack of the Theocrats!: How the Religious Right Harms Us All — and What We Can Do About It*, Sean Faircloth, Pitchstone Publishing, Charlottesville, Virginia @ 2012, p. 52.)

"I don't want to revert to the Dark Ages. And although I don't believe that homosexual people should be classified as a 'special' or 'protected' class of people, I am not a homophobe. I simply do not believe that changing the definition of marriage benefits society.

Changing the definition really shows a lack of understanding for what marriage is and what it isn't. Since the age of no-fault divorce, our legal system has sought to undermine the state of marriage and since the legalization of abortion (yes, I am a practicing Catholic, please don't roll your eyes at me and discount my perspective because I am not 'pro-choice'), our culture had really devalued the roles of mother, father and status of the unborn child. I want a strong culture with strong values which do not morph and blow this way and that way in the wind."

"This is a seismic change to our social fabric, one I really don't think is understood by those who are willing to rush into this and throw away or further trash a centuries old institution."

McCoy: The road ahead will be a difficult. Robert Fitzgerald Kennedy said, "Some men see things as they are and ask why? Others see things as they never were and ask why not?" Why not same-sex marriage? Why not give everyone equal civil rights?

———————

McCoy — From a pastor who is, I'm certain, an exemplar of Christian values:

"The truth is that social science demonstrates time and again that children who are raised by the married biological parents do better, live happier lives, and contribute more to society than the children of any other family configuration."

———————

McCoy: Citizens e-mailed senators urging them to sign a marriage petition proposed by Senator David Johnson for the right to vote. This e-mail was sent to seven other legislators, but not to me. However, I was not totally overlooked. The writer throws a sexual slur directly at me.

"You *(addressing another State Senator)* are back to your old slimy tricks and my wife saw firsthand how you refuse to answer simple questions and skirt the issue with a smoke screen. You are a master at that from many years of deceitful practice. You knew what they were speaking of (the petition for the right to vote) and you had seen it because Senator David Johnson presented it to each one of you Democrats except maybe *Matt McQueer*. All of the dictator's *(referring to Majority Leader Gronstal)* soldiers refused to sign the petition, including you, that would allow for a vote of the people to come to the Senate floor. You need to retire and let an honorable individual do the job we entrust to a Senator. I tried to be nice but is hard when I realize the poor leadership we have in the ultra democratic queer bought and paid for legislature."

———————

McCoy: Twenty years ago Michael Nava & Robert Dawidoff listed the following as the basic argument for equal rights for gays:

"1. The purpose of American constitutional government is the protection of individual rights.

2. Gays and lesbians, as American citizens, are entitled to the exercise of those rights.

3. Demonstrably, they are denied free exercise of those rights.

4. The grounds given for denying gays and lesbians their rights are rooted in ignorance and bias.

5. The organized opponents of gay rights, who exploit this ignorance and bias, would substitute sectarian religious morality in place of constitutional guarantees that allow individuals to determine how best to live their lives.

6. These forces are using the issue of gay rights as a test case in order to promote a broader agenda, the purpose of which is to limit individuality itself." (*Created Equal: Why Gay rights Matter to America*, Michael Nava & Robert Dawidoff, St. Martin's Press, New York, p. xii, 1994)

McCoy: Although significant progress has and is being made in achieving equal civil rights, the above arguments still remain very contemporary as evidenced by the number of states that have voted to prohibit same-sex marriage.

"We do not believe marriage is simply a private relationship between two people. Please let me know how you plan to address this issue."

McCoy: I have been very vocal in stating my support of marriage equality and have never wavered in my support of equal rights for everyone.

McCoy: Measuring what silent people think is hard to ascertain. I've never been able to do that with much assurance of accuracy. However, that wasn't a problem for some of my correspondents.

"People of Iowa have stated over and over that we, 'the silent majority,' are opposed to same sex marriage. Why can't the Polk County Attorney appeal the decision to the Supreme Court?"

"Please do not let six couples' decision to live a homosexual lifestyle trump the decisions of millions who believe and LIVE the truth that marriage is between one man and one woman."

McCoy: "Lifestyle" refers to the way a person chooses to live. It's a standard of living. Branding "gay" as a lifestyle is insinuating that it is like choosing a car. In the same manner one chooses to be gay. I simply would ask the writer, "When did you make the choice to be heterosexual?"

"I implore you to consider the damage that will be done to American, if not all, society by the decision of these few judges that would re-define marriage in Iowa. I encourage you to convince the governor to remove these judges from their positions and replace them with citizens who have not lost their moral compass."

McCoy: The governor has no constitutional or legal authority to remove judges.

"As parents we say don't mess with our kids! We know once legal the gay agenda pushes normalization in society and in school that will mean teaching to K-12 this is an okay 'normal' way to live. The gay lifestyle is anything but normal. I see us headed in a devastating direction; please do what you can to stem the tide. If we do not receive your help, please don't get too comfortable in your current position."

McCoy: This comment represented a form of fear mongering that simply isn't based in reality. "Our fears are so much greater than the reality of our experience." (*Gay Fathers*, Robert L. Barret & Bryan E. Robinson, p. 104, Jossey-Bass, A Wiley Company, San Francisco, @ 2000.)

"PLEASE protect our Iowa values and morals by voting to protect marriage in Iowa. The media is trying to divert attention from this atrocity by claiming it will bring economic strides to our state. However, to boost the Iowa economy by stooping to such a level as changing the laws to accept the sacrament of marriage between anything other than a man and a woman is downright shameful. More importantly, what am I supposed to tell my children and grandchildren when they ask, 'Why did this happen?'"

McCoy: Tell your grandchildren that Iowa has a proud tradition of extending civil rights and legal protections to all of its citizens. They might be proud of you if you stood up for that tradition as a champion of human rights ensuring that all share in the same freedoms. In doing so, you can tell them you made a difference.

"I believe that all people should enjoy the basic, inalienable rights on which the freedom of this country is based. However, law legalizes an action that has not truly been illegal. People in a same-sex union have never been denied these basic human rights. They receive no benefits from this law that they would not already possess through the power of attorney."

McCoy: Well, I wish it were that simple. In reality, same sex couples are denied over 1,100 benefits from the Federal Government enjoyed by married couples.

———————

"I was extremely disappointed that you voted against allowing the same sex marriage debate to come to the floor and be debated. Can you please explain why you did not feel it was a matter worth debating? Changing a law that has been a cornerstone of civilized society for thousands of years is a pretty radical move, and this recent ruling certainly was NEVER the intent of the founding fathers."

McCoy: I voted against writing discrimination into the Iowa Constitution. There has never been an Iowa constitutional question before voters which permits blatant discrimination and codifies it in our constitution.

———————

"Hi! I just sent this note to Governor Culver and thought you should see it as well *(e-mailed to 52 legislators on April 14, 2009)*:

There's some small aspect to the court's SSM (same sex marriage) that I don't think you've thought through — and this is just one example of why you desperately need to demand the time to think through the implementation of this ruling — about a year would be appropriate.

What about magistrates whose religious convictions will not allow them to perform same-sex marriages? Will you discriminate against them for their religious beliefs and tell them to perform same-sex marriages or quit, or will you allow an accommodation based on religious grounds?"

McCoy: The Governor has no authority to delay implementation of the Supreme Court's ruling. The Attorney General provided county clerks a month to get appropriate documents ready for same gender-marriages.

———————

"I am a resident of your district and understand that you are an openly gay person. The position the Democratic Party has taken on gay marriage must be a challenging issue for you to deal with. You must understand, right or wrong, that the people of Iowa have voted and spoken on this issue and you must protect our vote. You, as a member of the Democratic Party, have compromised your integrity in order to satisfy your own personal agenda. Our trust has been diminished and violated by non-elected Iowa Supreme Court. The people must have a fair opportunity to protect the vote that was cast a decade ago. If you continue to neglect the word or the majority of Iowa residents who voted for you then you will be defeated in your next election — you can count on that."

McCoy — I replied: "I'm patently insulted by your comments."

———————

"I urge you to do everything in your power to pass a residency requirement so that only Iowa gay couples can marry in our state. It is estimated that by the time a Marriage Amendment would be in effect, 58,000 homosexual couples would marry in Iowa. Of those people, 55,000 would be from other states. Therefore, in the best interest of our great state and country pass a residency requirement."

McCoy: Those numbers coming into Iowa would certainly have boosted our economy. But, it didn't happen. In fact, the masses of Iowans rushing to be married didn't materialize. The Iowa Vital Stats Department reported for the years 2009-2012 that 5,926 same-gender couples' marriages took place. Of that number, 1,853 were from Iowa and 4,073 were from out-of-state. The Department reported the numbers are

undoubtedly higher for same-sex marriages as they do not require applicants to state their gender. After our neighbors to the north approved marriage equality, the Minnesota governor advertised in Illinois and surrounding states for same-gender couples to come to Minnesota to be married. This resulted in an editorial in *The Des Moines Register* asking why Iowa had not conducted similar promotions to increase money coming into the state that would most have likely increased employment.

—————

"Homosexuality is a psychological disorder that is acquired in early childhood due to faulty bonding and identification with the same-sex parent. It indicates gender self-alienation and is preventable and treatable. It is not comparable to sex or race which cannot be changed." (Washington, D.C.)

McCoy: This writer needs to update his psychology book. In 1974 the American Psychiatric Association no longer considered homosexuality to be a mental illness.

—————

"Those of you that think the Supreme Court is sovereign and has the final authority in this matter should read the State Constitution and not allow yourself, and us, to be run over by the Court."

McCoy — I e-mailed back: "I am in receipt of your e-mail. You will have a chance to vote in the next election and it is your right to work to elect anti-equality candidates to the legislature who will work hard to pass a constitutional amendment to ban gay marriage. You see, the will of the people is expressed through the election process and your current legislature does not wish to alter or amend the Constitution. I would encourage you, or others who feel similarly, to make your case to the public and run for the legislature.

McCoy — The writer answered:

"Just curious, if one's sexual propensity is what defines people as a class to be protected under the Constitution, than does any person's sexual propensity, whatever that may be, qualify them for equal protection and granted the right of marriage in your view?"

McCoy — I wrote back to my pen pal: Please re-read your e-mail. Is this what you meant to write? Please clarify. Equal protection under the law is the basis for the Court's decision. Sexual orientation is a protected enumerated class under the civil rights protection of both Iowa and the City of Des Moines. Anyone of the specific enumerated classes of individuals would be covered under the Equal Protection Clause of the Constitution. Thank you for your e-mail.

McCoy — To which my pen pal responded:

"My world view is mostly shaped by my faith as a Christian. One can approach the Bible from one of two ways. As God's inspired word to mankind, kind of an instruction book on how He would have us live our lives, or more as a smorgasbord of ideas where we can take what we want and ignore what we don't. I subscribe to the first approach. I don't always like what God's word says, especially if it speaks to something that I may do that goes contrary to it. But I believe that His word is objective truth. So when God's word lists certain things as sexual sin then I believe that they are. Homosexual behavior is listed in the Bible right along with adultery, prostitution and fornication. All are listed as sexual immorality. None is any better or any worse than the others. My problem is with making anything a 'protected class' defined by one's sexual behavior or desires. The logic that follows the argument that homosexual activists have used, that God created them the way they are so they deserve to be a protected class because of their sexual orientation, then cannot the same argument be applied to anyone's sexual preference regardless of what it may be?

You sound like a nice guy but we are looking through two different world views The dictionary defines sodomy as 'sexual intercourse that is not the union of the genital organs of a man and a woman. The term is most frequently applied to anal intercourse between two men.' To be politically correct we most often use the phrase 'same-sex marriage' or 'homosexual marriage' or 'gay marriage,' but the fact of the matter remains that what we are talking about is 'sodomite marriage.' Don't be offended, but the word simply defines a behavior. When we talk about 'same sex marriage' in Iowa, what we are really talking about is legitimatizing sodomy by allowing two sodomites to get married."

Ferguson: I attended a dinner party where the conversation turned to gay marriage. An older lady said she had nothing against gays but was nauseated when she thought about the disgusting, degrading things they did to each other. Her much more accepting daughter suggested, "Well then mom, don't think about it." I was tempted to point out that many straight couples, especially younger couples, have not only copied gay's fashion styles but are also copying their sexual activities. But, I thought better of it and remained silent.

McCoy — I wrote the following to someone not living in my district: Throughout the State of Iowa and across the nation, citizens have been celebrating the unanimous decision of the Iowa Supreme Court, which upheld Judge Hansen's ruling in the Varnum vs. Brien decision. In a strongly written opinion the court stated the existing law violated individual's rights to equal protection and due process under our State's Constitution. I received the following response:

"You're joking right? Have you not heard the outcry of 'LET US VOTE" in front of the State Capitol? What part of this do you not understand? Or is this a matter of selective hearing where you only hear what you and the Democratic members of the General Assembly want to hear?

There is nothing to celebrate about the voices of the people being silenced! Nothing at all. In fact, this attempt at silencing the voices of Iowa's voters is one of the most shameful examples of partisan politics I've seen in recent memory. It is precisely this lack of responsiveness that caused me to resign from the Democratic National Committee a few months ago and to register as a Republican last week. I was a Democrat for over 36 years who never ONCE voted for a Republican. I walked precincts and manned the phones and stuffed envelopes election after election for Democratic candidates."

"Dear Mr. McCoy, it saddens me to read what you have written. Apparently, you've heard completely different reports than myself. That Supreme Court ruling has not been overwhelmingly received favorable, and the majority of Americans do not support it. We are not saying we do not love the gay people, because we do, but we are saying we do not support the act they are choosing to live."

McCoy: A Day of Silence was sponsored by One Iowa and GLSEN (Gay, Lesbian, & Straight Education Network), to protest bullying and harassment of gays in schools. Participating students spent the day in silence. The event actually began around 1996 at the University of Virginia and has spread to middle schools and high schools throughout the country. I spoke on the floor of the Iowa Senate asking senators to participate in a moment of silence in observance of the day as well as in memory of a gay Iowa high school student who had recently taken his own life because of having been bullied in school.

"How DARE you use your position in the Iowa Legislature to lodge into a tirade of hate speech against Chuck Hurley, a former Iowa legislator, for offering options to families as to how they could deal with this inappropriate Day of Silence being promoted in local schools. Gay and lesbian students already have more protections under law than Christian students. There are no laws that specifically prevent bullying against kids who carry Bibles or even against very overweight students. How DARE you think it's acceptable to single out gay and lesbian students for special treatment.

Personally, I think YOU'RE the one who needs to remain silent for a day. I seriously hope you'll do that. You and the rest of your legislators should be ashamed of yourselves for being bullied into standing up for this discriminatory, manipulative Day of Silence. I know you thought you were standing up to honor the life of one victim of hatred. Although we all respect that and should feel shame that this happened, the people of Iowa do not and will not respect your supporting the intentional manipulation of school-age children by such tactics as the Day of Silence. You all know better.

But above all, Mr. McCoy, you just don't get to use this stupid, pitiful stunt to try to bully the legislature into silencing the voters of Iowa on the gay marriage issue. You just aren't going to get away with that — at least not without people like me calling you on it. Personally, I really don't care about your lifestyle. I DO care when you push your lifestyle front and center into the business of the Iowa Legislature. STOP THAT, please. It's unprofessional it's inappropriate, and it is that kind of behavior — not your lifestyle — of representing your own personal agenda rather than representing the people of Iowa, that I hope loses you your career in public service. Let the people of Iowa vote! And by the way, that's not hate speech, it's Democracy 101."

McCoy: Such opposition strengthened my resolve to move forward for equality for all. Prevention of bullying in school is not limited to gay children, but would include any act of

harassment of individuals who possess certain characteristics which are then used as a source for bullying fellow students in schools. This would include students who carry Bibles.

Denying gays marriage licenses violated their constitutional rights, but the Polk County Attorney appealed the ruling to the Iowa Supreme Court. The Iowa Supreme Court said the law excluding gay and lesbian people from civil marriage has no relationship to any important governmental objective and concluded that the statute must be stricken from the Iowa Code. The Court ruled that the state's current marriage law violated the Iowa Constitution's Equal Protection Clause because the state cannot make laws that treat classes of people differently without a compelling reason.

The Court wisely acknowledged opposition from some religions to same-sex marriage, stating in its ruling, "Religious doctrine and views contrary to this principle of law are unaffected, and people can continue to associate with the religion that best reflects their views." A religious denomination can still define marriage as a union between a man and a woman, and a marriage ceremony performed by a minister, priest, rabbi, or other person ordained or designated as a leader of the person's religious faith does not lose its meaning as a sacrament or other religious institution. The sanctity of all religious marriages celebrated in the future will have the same meaning as those celebrated in the past. To implement the changes required by the Court's decision, the Attorney General worked with state and local officials to ensure appropriate procedures were in place when the Court's decision became effective on April 27, 2009.

"We have a right to vote on such an important issue as same sex-marriage!!! The only reason that I can see that it is being slipped under the rug is BIG MONEY and Power Politics!! I am telling you that the citizens of Iowa are angry!!!! YOU work for us. We are the ones footing the bills of our state and I highly advise you to get an amendment in order for the citizens to vote on. I will be waiting!! This is supposed to be a democracy! We will be counting on you!!!!"

——— ——— ———

McCoy: Not all correspondents played nice. Westboro Baptist Church, Topeka, Kansas, is known for its extreme ideologies. Under the guise of a "church" it is a small homophobic, anti-Semitic hate group. It's leader, Fred Phelps, was in Des Moines on April 24, 2009.

"Fags Can Marry, Sill! We were there when they let the fag flag be flown on that Capitol, and each other time Iowa did some insane, flagrant sinning contrary to their own interest.

We might as well be there when they do this bit of silliness. It is just lovely to see how God mocks them. They think they are mocking God, but God mocks them: Galatians 6:7 'Be not deceived; God is not mocked: for what so ever a man sows, that shall he also reap.' Proverb1:26 'I also will laugh at your calamity; I will mock when your fear cometh.' Just hold on you silly pushy fags. Pretty soon the last thing in this world you are going to be worried about is getting married one-to-another. You will be more concerned with having food, clothing and shelter as God continues to take your jobs and destroy your economy. You will only be under the same roof with someone else so you can try to consume them in their sleep. That's RIGHT, under Beast Obama, you will eat your children — or, er, um the adopted children some dumb ass social service worker allowed you to adopt. AMEN."

——— ——— ———

McCoy: Some writers seemed to take joy in prophesying doom and gloom. I'm certain they wallow in their selfish self-despair.

"I am sickened by the turn of events in our state. We do not have the power to change the laws of God in regards to marriage and I am asking you to let the people of Iowa vote. We are on the road to allowing Iowa to become the next Sodom and Gomorrah."

McCoy: Two posters at a rally for marriage equality that I particularly liked read, "Our love can't be voted away," and "'Justice' doesn't mean 'just us.'"

"I am disgusted by the arrogance of our Iowa Supreme Court judges to even think that they are superior enough to tell the people of Iowa what we want. I don't want to live in a state that allows homosexuals to have a marital status. I think they have enough rights with their sexual perversions that they should be happy that it's even tolerated."

McCoy: Bidstrup wrote in *At Issue: Gay Marriage* (ISBN15606924 Sept. 1998) "Many people continue to believe the propaganda from right-wing religious organizations that homosexuality is about nothing but sex, considering it to be merely a sexual perversion. The reality is that homosexuality is multidimensional, and is much more about love and affection than it is about sex...Sex, in a committed gay relationship, is merely a means of expressing that love, just the same as it is in heterosexual relationships. Being gay is much more profound than simply a sexual relationship; being gay is part of that person's core identity, and goes right the very center of their being."

"I think gays should have something like unions, with same status as normal weddings, but that is it, they are not natural and children do not have a choice and should not be in an un-natural place. Gays are adults and can make their own choice, but should not force it on minor children it is not a natural life."

McCoy: The writer is very comfortable intruding on the privacy of gay couples. I wonder if the writer is as bold with intrusion in the bedrooms of straight couples?

McCoy: Many writers against marriage equality were polite as well as civil.

"Please let me know how you plan to address this issue. Thank you for your consideration and your service to the State of Iowa."

"The people of Iowa voted you into office as representative of them. There are about two percent of Americans who are homosexual or gay/lesbian people. You should not let two percent of the population determine how to change a definition of marriage that has been supported by every culture and religion for 5,000 years. I ask that you begin representing the majority of this fine state and do what is right for them!"

McCoy: Our democracy does not, and should never allow the majority to take away the rights of the minority. I believe that the correct percentage of gays in the population is much closer to ten percent. When you factor in those people that identify themselves as bi-sexual that figure escalates. Check your history regarding every culture for 5,000 years supporting traditional marriage. Your statement is simply not accurate.

McCoy: Now and then a writer cited their academic credentials. I suspect to enhance the value of their opinion.

"I am a graduate from The University of Iowa. Please allow the citizens of Iowa to vote on a marriage amendment. This vote is needed because it fundamentally determines the 'brand' our state will project within the nation. This issue sets the future regarding our values, family structure, equality, marital rights and other key components vital to our society. Whether you are for or against the amendment, closure is necessary."

McCoy: Misunderstanding of the role of elected officials was a recurring theme. It's understandable. The role of an elected state senator is to represent their constituents as they act in the best interest of the state. It is not to represent the majority of Iowans as is the role of a United States senator.

"I am deeply disappointed in your position on this issue. This is a disgrace and an embarrassment to Iowa. You are clearly deciding to not do your job. Your job is to speak for the majority of Iowans. Is that what you are doing? You are allowing the misguided opinions of a select few to change Iowa law. You are clearly not upholding family values.

Peter Heck states, 'Physically, the consequences of homosexuality are devastatingly apparent. According to the *Omega Journal of Death and Dying*, the median age of death for homosexual men is between 40 and 43. The median age of death for heterosexuals is between 74 and 80. According to the Center for Disease Control homosexuals accounted for nearly 65% of all new HIV cases in 2003. Heck asks how someone, knowing these crippling physical, psychological, and spiritual consequences of the homosexual lifestyle, can encourage a person to embrace it. Is that loving? Urging people to engage in risky behavior that may leave them dead at nearly half the age of the general population is an odd definition of love in my book. Senator, why would you celebrate behavior that tears families apart, wrecks homes and sentences people to a lifetime of confusion, disease, and heartache?"

McCoy: Actually, the opposite would probably take place. The writer has to be aware that in a monogamous relationship (traditional marriages), the straight couples supposedly will not be engaging in risky behavior. The couple no longer engages in the dating or cruising scene with multiple sexual partners that might result in the spread of sexually transmitted diseases. This will probably be the same for committed same-sex couples. It is incumbent upon all participants who engage in sexual practices to observe and fully commit to safe sex behavior and practices.

"Your personal view about marriage is not relevant. We ask that you represent us, the voters, and stop homosexual marriages. The Supreme Court is out of control."

"It seems to be very discriminatory to define marriage as between 'a man and a woman or a man and a man or a woman and a woman.' If you are going to redefine marriage to be about LOVE and EQUALITY then marriage should include any UNION that one or MORE parties wants to be involved in. I know a very kind and loving man who wants to marry and take responsibility for more than one woman, shouldn't he also have the right to MARRY who he wants? Please re-write your law to include my friend's situation."

McCoy: This writer surprised me. He didn't quote the Bible to justify changing laws to allow polygamy.

"Why should we worry about HIV? It's a disease of choice. You don't make the wrong choice bingo you're healthy. So I say take all the HIV research money and apply it to more cancer research where you don't have a choice to abstain."

McCoy: The writer is blaming the victim. This is like saying cancer is a disease of choice for smokers or that heart disease is a choice of ignoring weight control and exercise.

"I have no problem with people being treated fairly. It is obvious to me you have another agenda than being fair. Gays and lesbians can be treated fairly without calling their 'unions' marriage. Sorry, but not buying what you're selling."

"I deeply resent the fact that our elected representatives do not feel we have the right and/or obligation to state our views in the voting booth. Quit treating us like a bunch of Mountain Willies and LET THE PEOPLE SPEAK!"

"We are watching. Those who will not oppose gay marriage will be voted out. I urge you to examine the Christian beliefs this nation was founded on and gay marriage must be stopped."

McCoy: Marriage equality is marriage for all — equal rights for all. Our nation was founded by some individuals who left England because of religious persecution. To claim that our national beliefs were Christian is not only inaccurate but deceptive.

"Thanks for letting me know where you stand. I will remember this when it is time for re-election."

"REMOVE HIM (*Senate Majority Leader Gronstal*) NOW!!! Democracy is gone in this State! Gronstal is a dictator! Any elected official who denies the people their right to vote must be removed from their position of leadership and power!

THIS IS AN OUTRAGE THAT THIS IS BEING ALLOWED TO HAPPEN !! I WAS OUT ON MY ROUNDS TODAY AND YOU WOULD NOT BELIEVE THE OUTRAGE OVER THIS. REMOVE THIS MAN FROM MAJORITY LEADER NOW!!!"

McCoy: Senator Mike Gronstal was re-elected by 55% of the vote in a Republican district. Well over $310,000 was poured into his opponent's campaign from out of state sources in hopes of ousting him.

"I don't really care what the rest of the nation thinks, the vast majority of your constituents are against this. If you are not there to represent us then my prayer would be that you are replaced in the next election by someone who will be there to represent Iowans and not the special interest of gay lobbies. You should be ashamed of your dereliction of duty to the citizens of Iowa."

"I am appalled that you, as a member of the majority Democratic Party, are stonewalling a constitutional amendment regarding the same sex marriage fiasco. You're supposed to represent all Iowans, not just your far left liberal base. You did not listen to the Iowan's protesting with the Tea Party yesterday. People are angry. I don't remember the level of arrogance you and other Democrats project at not representing the majority of all Iowans. My family and circle of friends, regardless of party of affiliation, will certainly hope that you're not re-elected."

McCoy: The following was sent to Senator Gronstal and copied to me.

"It is not your place to play 'God' and decree the residents of Iowa have no right to determine how marriage is defined in this state. From what I saw and heard you say in the news smacks of arrogance. You seem to forget, we pay your wages and you are representing all of Iowa. This is not a 'screw you' state. I doubt if you will acknowledge this with anything other than a boilerplate generic 'thank you for writing.'"

"What are _you_ doing under the Gold Dome???? You've got hours left to make the right decisions and positive impact — consider for once doing the RIGHT THING! I'd rather say, 'Thank you' than 'Shame on you!' And right now, I'm leaning towards 'Shame.'"

McCoy: The corrosive power of fear is evident in this e-mail.

"These types of actions will ruin our wonderful state not to mention our country's heritage. YOU are forgetting about the children subject to this unnatural arrangement. You may want to change our classroom education in regard to 'where do babies come from.' I am confident my daughter will not understand how her classmate's same sex parents have a child after studying human anatomy 101."

McCoy: The Iowa Supreme Court's decision is about making sure that all Iowans are treated fairly. Iowa has a long and proud tradition of assuring the basic rights and protections of all Iowans including integration and women's right to vote. Iowa courts have been leaders in extending necessary rights and protections to Iowans. In Iowa we treat each other fairly. It is only fair that two committed loving people should be able to take full responsibility for each other. No civil rights issues have been easy to advance without some opposition. This has been consistent throughout history.

"This debate is not about fairness, equality, or any other fuzzy term liberals like to give it. It is about who gets a tax break. It is about pushing an agenda. No one cares what anybody else does with their body parts, or who they love, or who they want to leave their life savings to. But why should two people who cannot contribute to the future of our society be given a discount when single people aren't? Why is it not enough for them to just claim their dependents as credits? Maybe it would be if it wasn't for the mentality that everybody in the country has to accept what they like to do naked before they will feel that Americans are tolerant."

"How dare you compare what someone does in their bedroom to the suffering of African Americans or other inequalities that have taken place in history. Show me the gas chambers! Gays can vote, own their own home, visit their loved ones in the hospital, leave a life insurance policy to whomever they want, have sex with whomever they want, etc. But, they cannot, on a large scale, produce future tax payers to pay into their social security accounts when they are elderly. They cannot create little people who will be the future of this country. That is why they are not entitled to the same 'perks' as married people. If your argument is financial fairness, that is the difference. Your name is now on my list of individuals that I will do everything in my power to make sure you never hold public office in the state of Iowa again."

McCoy: I'm sure that my son might disagree with much of what you have said. As a side note, your reference to the gas chambers reminded me that at the beginning of the Holocaust, the first victims were gypsies and gays.

"I understand your misguided viewpoint, Mr. McCoy. But I didn't ask for your opinion, what I asked for is to allow the bill to be debated and put on a ballot. I simply think your viewpoint is wrong and honestly kind of scary. I know you really don't care about what most people think. That fact stands since you are in a minority in Iowa. I will NOT allow activist judges to hold hostage our balance of power and shame on you for allowing the judicial system to hold that kind of power over the legislature. That alone sets a scary precedent.

If you allow gays to marry, what comes next? I would like to have several wives, and if you want to make gay marriage a civil rights issue than polygamy is too, and so is a person wanting to marry their cousin or sister. If you allow gay marriage, those types of unions are soon to follow. You see, just because I want something doesn't make it right. Nor does it make it a civil right! You politicians should take a course on common sense! Your kind of progressive view point is not what we need in this state."

———————

"A marriage is a sexual and emotional bond between two humans of opposite sex. Homosexuals cannot participate in the intimate physical behavior that unites two heterosexual individuals emotionally. If you don't understand this, review your high school biology (hopefully you passed this course). I see this decision as an attack on the American family. I have been teaching high school for thirty years. I have never dealt with so many emotionally confused youth as I do today. Children today are so confused about their sexuality that they can't find emotional fulfillment. I am sickened by our state. I will make sure I campaign against you in our next election."

McCoy: It saddens me to think that someone who has spent thirty years teaching high school biology is so blatantly inaccurate in understanding human sexuality. Think about retiring from your profession so you will not subject more children to your ignorance.

———————

"ALLOWING SAME SEX MARRIAGE IS A DIRECT ATTACK ON ALL RELIGIONS. COURT COULD NOT HAVE TAKEN INTO ACCOUNT THE VERY NATURE OF HOMOSEXUALITY. HOMOSEXUALS ARE IN A GROUP LIKE ADULTERY, INCEST, RAPE AND ALL OTHER SINS OF THE FLESH. NO ONE WOULD THINK OF GIVING

SOME OTHER MINORITIES THESE RIGHTS. WE EXPECT THOSE WHO WRITE OUR LAWS TO HAVE GOOD MORALS BUT WHAT WE ARE GETTING ARE THOSE WHO HAVE NO MORALS AND ARE WORKING FOR INTERESTS FUNDED FROM OUT OF STATE."

———————

"When has the way a person chooses to have sex ever been defined as a 'civil right?' It makes absolutely no difference to me what two consenting adults do in the privacy of their home so long as no one is being harmed by it. But why is it necessary to drag that behavior into public and demand special rights for it? I'm sorry you don't see the rational side of this issue."

McCoy: Marriage equality is about "equal rights" not "special rights." Sexual intimacy is one aspect of marriage regardless of how marriage is defined. It is not the purpose of the union, but rather an expression of a healthy relationship.

———————

McCoy: Personal attacks were not uncommon.

"You seem to be on the minority side of the fence and are refusing to listen to opposing arguments because you are celebrating a victory. I don't understand. When you were first elected, you were married and had a family. That is what needs to be celebrated. You are supposed to be living in the area you represent. You are not. *(McCoy: I have always lived in the area which I represented.)* Usually there is money involved somewhere to form people's opinions on what side of the fence they are working. Where are you getting your election funding money? Why is this your allegiance? It wasn't true when you were running for election. You didn't win on a gay platform. By refusing to allow this to come to a vote, you are violating MY rights to a representative."

McCoy: All of my campaign contributions and expenses are public record and on file with the Campaign Ethics and Financial Disclosure Board.

——— ———

"I am angry that you are not standing up for the 62% of Iowans who disagree with same sex marriage. This is a very perilous time in our nation. I am sick of compromise. Stand up for what you believe! Quit falling into the trap of the politically correct. Of what are you afraid?"

McCoy: I have openly and strongly defended my beliefs. That is what is upsetting to you.

——— ———

"There are people all over this nation praying for you. Whether you believe it or not, God ordained marriage between a man and a woman at the beginning of time. The more we shake our fists at Him and dismiss Him from our nation, the more our nation and her economy will collapse."

McCoy: Clearly, our understanding and concept of God are different. My God is loving, and one that has made us in His image. Your concept of God as an enforcer and one who punishes his children is not something I easily grasp.

——— ———

"I believe the stance of each of the elected official's opinions should be in print so that I and others know what their stance is in 2010."

McCoy: Campaigns are intended to provide the candidate an opportunity to let voters know where they stand on issues and for voters to be able to question them in depth. I think it's a red flag, and borders on dishonesty, when a candidate avoids revealing where they come down on an issue.

——— ———

McCoy — Angry comments were frequent from the "Let us Vote" crowd expressing fanatically felt emotions:

"Are you a true representative of the people who voted you in office or one of those politicians who once elected, do your own thing? You think I am just one person out here with these crazy ideas? You better think again. I have never written such a message to our leaders before. I am just finally FED Up and cannot sit idly by while the elected officials we voted in office fail to listen to the majority of hard working, taxpaying decent citizens of the great state of Iowa. For those of you who want to look up my party affiliation, I will save you the time. You will find I am and always have been a registered Democrat and I vote in all elections."

———

"We have just started to become angry about this and I think you are going to be in trouble if you don't put it (*the vote*) to the people. ENOUGH IS ENOUGH!!! We are tired of you shoving things down our throats and we will do everything in our power to set things right!!!!! Everyone I talk to knew nothing about this going on including me. NOW WE WILL FIGHT YOU!!!!!"

———

"Don't let out-of-state wealthy activists determine the future of Iowa. If you have sold your soul there is still time to redeem it. Get some backbone, and stop enactment of one judge's illegal decision."

———

"Your outlook on our democratic system is disturbing. We the people of this state have the power, not you. You were elected by us, to serve us. It is a pretty shallow outlook to think only legislators have the power. You will find out shortly enough that the people hold the real power, and if you continue to be so power hungry and short sighted with your view points on government, you will no longer be privileged to serve us."

McCoy: My response to e-mailers that were especially angry or passionate in their cause was to encourage them to put themselves on the front line of involvement and run for office. I have always told individuals that democracy is hard work, start early.

"I know this is a long shot, knowing your views on the subject, but you are my senator and feel I must ask that you would vote to allow the Iowa Marriage Amendment out of committee and let the people vote on this issue."

McCoy: Lincoln's immortal words might be appropriate here, ". . . he who would *be* no slave, must consent to *have* no slave. Those who deny freedom to others, deserve it not for themselves; and, under a just God, cannot long retain it." (Lincoln, Abraham, *Letter to Henry L. Pierce and Others, The Collected Works of ABRAHAM LINCOLN*, Vol. III, Abraham Lincoln Association, Springfield, IL, Roy P. Basler, Editor, Rutgers University Press, New Brunswick, NJ, 1953, p. 376.)

"I am sick and tired of judges issuing opinions that legislators accept as law. The discussion came up last year and many of the legislators preferred waiting stating something to the effect 'let us just wait and see how the court rules.' Well, the court has ruled and NOW you are TAKING the RIGHTS of the PEOPLE OF IOWA away from them if you do not allow this legislation to be brought to a vote."

"Part of the reason we are in this budget mess is because of the moral decline in society. As I grew up, (I am 56) there was no need for ethics training because it was something we were taught and expected to live by. As social mores decline so did the ability of all of us to trust others. By not bringing this matter before the legislature, you are encouraging declining morals in Iowa."

"Yesterday was a sad day for Iowa. Now Iowa ranks right up there with Massachusetts and Connecticut as the only states that allow same-sex partners to apply for a marriage licenses. This is what happens when we allow money from out of state from the gay lobby to take over and use Iowa as a testing ground. This is only the beginning. Soon, preachers, ministers, and priests will be banned from preaching against homosexuality from the pulpit. Soon, our Christian adoption agencies across the state will be forced to recognize these same sex marriages and allow these couples to adopt children from their agencies."

McCoy: This is not true. In fact, no religious institution will be impacted in any way. This ruling will have no impact on a religious institution's teachings, values or practices. They are exempted from recognizing or performing same gender marriages.

"Please explain to me how you represented me. Why should you be re-elected? Your voting record and lack of communication are a problem."

McCoy: I am not sure I like the tone of your email. While I am elected to serve you, I don't think I am elected to serve as your whipping post. For the record, I send a weekly newsletter while the legislature is in session. I have consistently, every other week, added names of any one that has requested to receive my newsletter. I have more than 3,100 constituents to whom I provide weekly updates via e-mail. I publish a bi-weekly column in our state newspaper, the *Des Moines Register,* where I publish my contact information. This past session, I have responded throughout session personally, in most cases, to thousands of phone calls and e-mails from constituents. I have published my home

phone number and cell phone number for my constituents to call me day or night. I held three listening posts on Saturday mornings in my district. I have attended 21 public meetings during session and six neighborhood meetings.

"On Friday, April 3, 2009, the Iowa Supreme Court voted UNANIMOUSLY to allow the recognition of licensed homosexual and lesbian marriages in the state of Iowa. You promised Iowans that you would stand against this move, now however you are changing your positions. We will hold you to your words, your vows upon being elected. Couples will flock to Iowa for their 'marriage' and then go back to their home states and demand equal rights with other married couples in the workplace, hospitals, etc. This causes chaos and departure from our basic beliefs. Where is our freedom?" (Minnesota resident)

McCoy: I have never changed my position on support of equal civil rights for all. Never have I promised to vote against the state constitution. And, I certainly didn't promise anything to you, a resident of Minnesota.

"This is not a civil issue, it is a MORAL issue. It is not about being treated fairly, it is about wholesomeness in families that allows for a mother and a father for children. If two people want to take care of each other they don't need a marriage license to do it. The judicial system is overriding the desire of the majority and misrepresenting their constituents, abusing their power – nothing equal about that."

McCoy: You claim that two people living together don't need a marriage license, then why bother with marriage for either heterosexual or homosexual couples? This is a moral issue and moral arguments can be very strong. The problem is that people's moral compasses vary greatly.

"I am NOT proud of Iowa being the third state in the union where gay marriage is legal. I am sick and tired of having the courts dictate to the majority what the minority wants. As soon as I get one, I am going to start flying the 'Don't Tread on Me' flag. It is an abomination, what has just been shoved down our throats of your constituents."

McCoy: Look back through history to see if you really want to be identified with those that have opposed civil rights — equal rights — for all citizens.

———•———

"I will NOT be voting for you ever again. I will be campaigning and voting for whoever runs against you. You have become too liberal for the beliefs that I have which come from the Bible. I'm sorry that you have SOLD OUT to a belief that is NOTHING MORE THAN A LIE! It is time that the Political Class in the state be replaced with people who will listen to the will of the people. You have been put on notice. Enjoy your last term as Senator."

McCoy: This wasn't quite my last term. I was re-elected the next time around, Nov. 2012, by a very large majority. In 2014 I did not have an opponent.

———•———

"Well, I have finally seen it all. There has been a total destruction of the state of marriage in the state of Iowa. Aren't there any Democrats that are outraged at what is happening? If I were a Democrat, I would today become a Republican and do all I could to stop this total out of control Democratic leadership from ruining what is left of this state."

———•———

"There is no established religion that recognizes same-sex marriage as its official view. Since our judicial branch has no authority to enact new law — our elected legislature simply MUST ACT before this session is adjourned. To 'do nothing' and allow their ruling to stand — you would be going against EVERY religion in the U.S.A. Even the pre-amble of our State's Constitution recognizes THE Supreme Being — (God) as having supreme authority over us all. Don't be so arrogant to think you can ignore HIM, and that He won't judge us as a result. There IS supreme truth — and it does not come from judges — it comes from our Almighty God, and Creator only."

McCoy: Clearly this is a good time to remember there is separation between church and state. No organized religion is required to recognize same-gender marriage.

McCoy: Writers sometimes jump to unwarranted conclusions in their scolding.

"So you believe that a brother and a sister who are loving and committed should be allowed to get married? What about a single mother and her 25 year old son? By your reasoning they should also be allowed to get married."

McCoy: A writer from North Carolina was less than pleased with me.

"How disappointed to see that supreme court judges in your state are making law instead of upholding law. I am angry that you are not standing up for the 62% of Iowans who disagree with same sex marriage. This is a very perilous time in our nation. I am sick of compromise. Stand up for what you believe! Quit falling into the trap of the politically correct. Of what are you afraid? Whether you believe it or not, God ordained marriage between a man and a woman at the beginning of time. The more we shake our fists at Him and dismiss Him from our nation, the more our nation and her economy will collapse." (North Carolina)

McCoy: The judges did not make new law. They upheld the constitution by striking down a ban on same-gender marriage as unconstitutional. In doing so they upheld our constitution's equal protection clause which is apparently what you wanted them to do. Courts do not create rights not found in the constitution. "Compromise" is at the heart of making a democracy work. It is absolutely necessary and if we had more of it in government we'd have less gridlock.

————————

"The recent irresponsible court decision is that now Iowa has discriminated against all its citizens where before all citizens were free to marry members of the opposite sex, with few restrictions. With this new ruling that purportedly ends discrimination against homosexuals, we are faced with almost infinite possibilities to discriminate against all possibilities of classes that one might devise i.e. sisters and brothers, mothers and sons, pets and owners, polygamy, plural groups, etc., etc., etc. The decision of the court has not made us freer as a people, but has worked a terrible injustice with the consequence we shall become further enslaved. The ruling by the Iowa Supreme Court is out of touch with Iowans. It does a grave injustice to further damage an already reeling society."

McCoy: This is unexplainable silliness.

————————

"It would be a grave moment if I ever voted Republican, but I know I won't be voting for you next time around!"

————————

"If Majority Leader Gronstal refuses to allow debate on this issue to come to the floor of the Senate because of his fear of what the people of Iowa would decide if given the right to vote on how marriage is to be defined in Iowa, then those of you who are in the same party and have placed him in that position of leadership need to vote him out of that position and replace him with someone who is not afraid to allow the people of Iowa's voice to be heard."

———

"I demand that you uphold the voice of your people and oppose the decisions made by these judges. Though I am a citizen of Michigan, I fear the implications that would be placed on my state if this was passed. This decision allows homosexuals in Michigan to 'marry' in Iowa and force legal acknowledgement of their 'marriage' in Michigan. I am upholding the morals for Michigan and I pray that you will do the same for your state." (Michigan)

McCoy: This is a nationwide movement for equal civil rights that will eventually include your state. I am proud Iowa is at the forefront of this historic event.

———

"Like you, I am happy with today's ruling. I do have to say though, I am disappointed, if the *Des Moines Register* is accurate in reporting your response as: "The God squad's coming in the door now." I'm not sure what you meant by that, but it seems intended to mock people of faith. I don't think it helps the cause to be disrespectful of others' beliefs. These kinds of statements only give others a reason to dismiss and despise."

McCoy: The folks I referred to were self-appointed Christians who were damning gays to hell and determining who was and was not saved.

———

McCoy: The following letter was originally e-mailed to Senator Michael Gronstal, Majority Leader of the Senate.

"I was very disheartened to read that you feel it is 'exceedingly unlikely' for you to bring the issue against same-sex marriage to our representatives in the legislature so that ALL the citizens of Iowa can have a voice through a vote. I even heard on the news that the Des Moines Convention Bureau felt it was great and would bring a lot of money in for the state of Iowa. Do we really need that? No!! I hope that you are a God fearing man Mr. Gronstal and that you will recall what happened in Sodom and Gomorrah when the people gave themselves over to their perverted lusts and greed. That is exactly what will happen to Iowa if we allow this immoral behavior to continue. I do understand that everyone says a vote cannot take place yet this year, but a moratorium can be placed and stop this immorality from desecrating our land. As an elected official you ARE obligated to do this for the people of Iowa and you can bet we will remember when all the representatives come up for re-election."

McCoy: The following e-mail was addressed to house representatives with a copy to senators for a total of 147 recipients.

"Sirs & Madams: Normally you should be addressed as Honorable Representatives, but I don't believe you have earned this courtesy. I am addressing you as a group that has become a big disappointment by the majority, we the people of Iowa. Please take the courtesy not to delete this, but read entirely and reflect on what is said.

The people of Iowa are pissed. Absolutely positively pissed. It appears we have no voice as no one is voicing our concerns. Our representatives seem to have lost their ethical backbone to stand up for us if they had one to begin with. And instead they are too afraid to fight in our defense. What's going on here? What is the real story? I know some of you may not agree with others, but damn it, say so and get a spine. I've never ever seen such spineless sponges in all my life, including the governor on this issue. The governor vowed to uphold Iowa's marriage laws between man and woman. He said this. We voted him in. Now he says he did not break any promises because this is a religious issue and churches can still have marriage between man and woman. Think on this…now not only did the governor not hold up to his promise, but his answer makes him hypocritical. The majority, we the people, agree no matter how it's fabricated, the rationale or how justified, a promise to Iowa has been broken. Our trust in you has failed. Smoke screens and camouflage were used to keep things away from us. The gays and lesbians that are our representatives: Are you representing yourself, your interests, or truly being unbiased and representing the majority?

The government is shutting down the people and as it continues there will be some modern form of a revolution to come. Not just in Iowa, but throughout the nation the people are sick and tired of government and what is going on. Government is here for the people, not the people here for the government. Just today at the barber shop was great discussion that we are past the drain and now swirling down the plumbing to be spewed out to the sewer. Now it's worse due to your ignorance of our need to rectify this issue, or to allow this to happen in the first place. Our morale is low. People who have been silent, thinking we are being represented correctly and now learned their representatives really are traitors, are getting ready to scream. Meanwhile, politicians think everything is just fine, content in being ignorant and living in a daydream. It is clear that payoffs have been made, contributions from gay activists and pro-abortionist accepted by politicians for campaign funds. It really is transparent to all. I'm telling you we the people are not stupid, we are not ignorant. We are just mad and fed-up. We have a memory and it would appear many of you need to be voted out. You're not doing your job in representing your constituents. We thank God your time is limited, and pray you don't destroy us until then.

No disrespect intended. I mean no harm or attack. My only intention is to make you boys and girls think about what you're doing to the majority of Iowans and how sick and tired we are of the power you have and abusing it. I am not on this earth to judge, for that is for a higher power, God. I do not flaunt my sexual preferences to others and I'd rather no one do that to me."

McCoy: You said, "No disrespect intended." None taken.

"I'm writing in regards to a statement you made to a friend in an e-mail reply to her regarding homosexual 'marriage.' You said, 'County recorders throughout Iowa have been directed by the Court to issue marriage licenses effective April 24, 2009.' With all due respect, sir, I fail to understand how this is acceptable. The courts ruled DOMA to be unlawful, but they did not make a new law. Right? That is your job. The courts tell us whether the laws are legal; they don't make the laws.

I am not a lawyer. I've simply studied government and business law. Even if they did direct the county recorders, what makes this order valid? From my angle, it appears the Iowa Supreme Court has thrown the ball back to you and your colleagues to fix what's broken in their opinions. They don't have the authority to fix it. Do they?"

McCoy: Yes the Supreme Court does has the authority to rule that an existing law, DOMA, is unconstitutional and strike it down. Additionally, they do have the authority to instruct county recorders to remedy this unconstitutional law by issuing marriage licenses to same gender couples.

"First off, I am going to get something off my chest. I don't like you and never will. You suck at what you are suppose to do. You impose your own opinion and views into politics and that is not your job. You are suppose to represent us as long as it is legal."

McCoy: I strongly believe that with this issue I do represent not only my constituents but the citizens of Iowa in refusing to vote discrimination into our constitution.

McCoy: As a recovering Catholic, I am well aware of the church's strong opposition to marriage equality. Pedophile priests have been allowed for years to have their way with young boys without sanctions by the Church. But, the good fathers are on high alert when it comes to same-sex marriage. Not certain how those two values are compatible. I don't know why they are afraid of same-gender marriage. If they don't want to perform same-gender marriages in their churches, they will get no argument from me. But don't actively advocate preventing marriage equality for everyone.

As I anticipated, St. Anthony Catholic Church and Christ the King Catholic Church, both located in my Senatorial District, took a strong stand against my support of same-gender marriage. St. Anthony's is the church where my family and I were long-time worshippers. I attended St. Anthony's grade school. The two churches took a strong stance against marriage equality. Their church memberships represent more than 6,000 of my constituents. The letters represent an effort by the priests to publically bully me by inserting them into their church bulletins for weekend masses in an attempt to get me to adopt their anti-marriage position. Their goal was to put me on notice that my failure to advocate for marriage equality would result in their opposing to me in the up-coming election. A series of civil letters were exchanged between the church and me. They follow.

Christt the King Catholic Church
5711 SW 9th • Des Moines, Iowa 50315-5006 • (515) 285-2888

February 22, 2008

Senator Matt McCoy
Iowa State Legislature
5016 Pleasant Street
Des Moines, IA 50312

Dear Senator McCoy::

Enclosed is an Open Letter which Monsignor Frank Chiodo, Pastor of St. Anthony's Parish and I have jointly composed, urging you to use your influence to bring the marriage amendment to a vote. We believe that this desire of ours represents the vast majority of our parishioners here on the south side of Des Moines. The Open Letter will appear as an insert in our Sunday bulletins this weekend.

Please know we will all appreciate your efforts to bring this amendment to a vote so that we can all express our opinions democratically at the polls on this critical social issue. Thank you for representing us in this matter.

Sincerely yours,

Rev. Msgr. Frank E. Bognanno

McCoy: The above letter from the Rev. Msgr. Bognanno was dated February 22, 2008 which was a Friday. The "Open Letter" from Bognanno and the Rev. Msgr. Frank Chiodo that follows was also dated February 22, 2008. It was to be distributed on Sunday, February 24, 2008 which left no time for anyone to voice objection to their stand or distribution. I responded to its writers on Monday, February 25, 2008. Both letters follow.

Christt the King Catholic Church
5711 SW 9th Des Moines. Iowa 50315-5006 (515) 285-2888 ,

St. Anthony Catholic Church
15 Indianola Rd. – Des Moines. Ia 50315
Phone: 515-244-4709 – Fax: 515-280-6959
www.stanthonydsm.org

OPEN LETTER
February 22, 2008

Senator Matt McCoy
Iowa State Legislature
State Capitol
Des Moines, IA 50309

Representative Bruce Hunter
House of Representatives
State Capitol
Des Moines, IA 50309

Dear Senator McCoy and Representative Hunter:

As you know, the Polk County District Court in 2007 struck down Iowa's law which ruled that only a marriage between a man and a woman is valid. This ruling is now on appeal to the Iowa Supreme Court.

The Iowa Family Policy Center survey indicates that over 70% of Iowans agree that marriage should only be between one man and one woman. In addition, the Des Moines Register recent survey of Iowa's Legislators indicated a distinct majority wishing to support an amendment to Iowa's Constitution upholding this traditional definition of marriage.

The Catholic Church is absolutely and unequivocally committed to the traditional understanding of the institution of marriage defined and practiced as a covenant between one man and one woman. The natural law, rooted in reason and common sense, clearly demonstrates that such a definition is indeed the fundamental pillar for a stable society.

Our two parishes of St. Anthony and Christ the King, totaling some 6,000 Catholic adults stand committed to preserving the institution of marriage as between one man and one woman. The family is the first and fundamental unit of society. All societies in history have legislated marriage as only between a man and a woman because of its unique contribution to the common good. Although good kids can come out of a variety of situations, children do best with a mother and father in the home.

If the Iowa Supreme Court does not reverse the District Court ruling then the door is open to redefining "marriage". This would make possible as a legal right all combinations of multiple men/men. women/women. men/several women (polygamy) relationships. Legalizing polygamy is now being voted on in some sectors of Canada where same-sex marriages are allowed. "Legal recognition of same sex unions of placing them on the same level as marriage would mean not only the approval of disordered behavior with the consequence of making it a model in present day society, but would also obscure basic values which belong to the common inheritance of humanity" (words of Pope John Paul II).

We know that amending Iowa's Constitution is difficult and should not be taken lightly. The only way to do so is to have two successive General Assemblies pass the legislation (in this case, in 2008 and 2009), which then would put the amendment to a vote of the people of Iowa. If the legislature doesn't act this year, the earliest date the people could vote is 2011.

Please contact your party's leadership and ask for a vote on a marriage amendment. Even if you do not agree on the need for this measure, we believe that the legislature should pass the amendment so that we, the people of your districts, can vote on an issue that is so critical. Please let us exercise our right to vote.

We would like to know how you plan to address this issue. Thank you for your consideration and your service to the State of Iowa.

Sincerely,

Rev. Msgr. Frank E. Bognanno
Pastor, Christ the King Church

Rev. Msgr. Frank Chiodo
Pastor, St. Anthony Church

MATT McCOY
STATE SENATOR
Twenty-first District
Polk County
Statehouse (515) 281-3371
matt.mccoy@legis.iowa.gov

ADDRESS
1717 Ingersoll Ave.
Suite 115
Des Moines, IA 50309

The Senate
State of Iowa
Eighty-fifth General Assembly
STATEHOUSE
Des Moines, IA 50319

ASSISTANT MAJORITY LEADER

COMMITTEES

Appropriations
Commerce, *Chair*
Government Oversight
State Government
Transportation
Ways and Means

Transportation, Infrastructure and Capitals
Appropriations Subcommittee, *Chair*

February 25, 2008

Rev. Msgr. Frank E. Bognanno
Chrit the King Catholic Church
15 Indianola Road
Des Moines, IA 50315

Rev. Msgr. Frank Chiodo
St. Anthony Catholic Church
5711 SW 9th Street
Des Moines, IA 50315

Dear: Msgr. Bognanno & Msgr. Chiodo:

PERSONAL & CONFIDENTIAL

Gentleman in response to your letter I received February 23, I want to acknowledge receipt of this letter. I was unclear as to what "OPEN LETTER" meant but I assume that this was distributed widely, since it has been issued to my colleagues in the Iowa Senate by Senator David Johnson.

Enclosed is a copy of an article on a survey by the *Des Moines Register* which ran on February 10, 2008. Apparently, you both must have missed that article. My constituents understand I am on record on this issue, as I have been very clear whenever this issue has been discussed.

Currently the Iowa Supreme Court is in the process of preparing to rule on Judge Hanson's summary judgment relating to marriage. I have always respected the three separate branches of government. I do not believe it is appropriate for the legislature to engage in this debate while this matter is pending before th Iowa Supreme Court. I trust this response satisfies your question of how I would vote.

I appreciate that reasonable people can disagree on this issue. Know that I will always stand on the side of resisting discriminations of all classes of people. I believe in the equal protection of all under the law. It is important to allow the courts to work free of legislative interference.

Sincerely,

Matt McCoy

Each day, on the floor of the Iowa Senate we have time for Senators to stand and make remarks about anything they wish. Senator David Johnson, a conservative senator, stood and spoke about wanting to have the right to vote on same-gender marriage. He referenced the open letters that were delivered by my parishes and said it was time to allow Iowans the right to vote.

Senator David Johnson seems to have been the mouthpiece for the Catholic Church. He could have been their poster boy on issues involving abortion, contraception and marriage equality. Johnson spent a lot of time around my former church, St. Anthony's, and formed a relationship with the priests from that parish. It is also important to note that Senator Johnson, who so proudly stood on the floor of the Iowa Senate defending marriage, has been married three times.

As a former Catholic, I must admit, I am never surprised by the hypocrisy of the Roman Catholic Church. As a child, I attended Catholic schools for my entire education including graduating from Briar Cliff University, a Catholic University. The same church that turns its back on gays and lesbians for their perceived imperfections is also the same organization that protects Catholic priests who have sexually abused young boys.

Not only did the church turn its head on child sexual abuse by clergy, the church participated in highly organized systematic cover-ups of that sexual abuse. This organization moved money and real estate to shield assets from law suits by abuse victims with the full consent of the Vatican.

As a young boy attending St. Anthony's School I dreamed that one day I might be a Catholic priest. St. Anthony's was my parish. I loved my faith and I loved my church. I never dreamed that I would end up ostracized by the church hierarchy. The church I loved condemned me and attacked me at a time I needed my faith the most.

Addressing One Iowa Rally on anniversary of the legalizing of marriage equality.

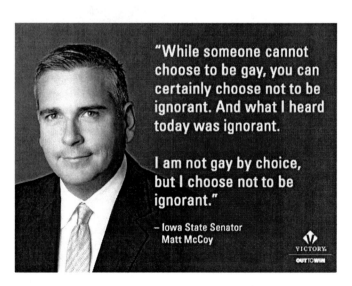

"While someone cannot choose to be gay, you can certainly choose not to be ignorant. And what I heard today was ignorant.

I am not gay by choice, but I choose not to be ignorant."

— Iowa State Senator Matt McCoy

VICTORY
OUT TO WIN

Victory Fund's poster went viral quoting me on the floor of the Iowa Senate defending marriage equality.

My son Jack and I at the rally to Celebrate Marriage Equality.

My family has provided me with strong support.

Pictured are my son Jack, me, my brother Pat, and my dad Bill McCoy at the rally to Celebrate Marriage Equality.

I attended the signing of the HIV Decriminalization Bill by Iowa Gov. Terry Branstad. I was instrumental in its passage with strong support from my assistant Christian Zenti who stands in the background immediately to my left.

At my desk in the Iowa State Senate.

I joined the We Are One rally at the Statehouse in support of public employees' right to bargain collectively for their pay and benefits.

Co-author Jim Ferguson with his wife Jill.

Chapter 4: Saint or Sinner McCoy, You Will Be Accountable to GOD for this ONE!

"Nothing can separate us from the love of Christ Jesus."

David Ruthe, Senior Minister Plymouth Congregational Church, Des Moines, Iowa

---

"Coming out is the most religious thing you can do. All who we are is on the line – God created us. Be your authentic-self."

Bishop Gene Robinson, retired bishop of the Diocese of New Hampshire,
Keynote speaker Interfaith Alliance of Iowa Awards Dinner, May 2, 2013.

It should not be a surprise to anyone that religious beliefs are foremost in a person's stance on same-sex marriage. People define their rules based upon *their* interpretation of the Bible or often how they have been *told* to interpret it. Arguments for and against same-gender marriage are supported by the same scripture and how it pertains to sexuality. Each side argues Bible verse-for-verse to prove they know what God really said about homosexuality and of course their interpretation is accurate. What people justify in the name of religion is because it's their particular religion.

Accurate interpretation of the Bible requires that it be understood within its historical context. A biblical scholar explained that laws in the Bible against same-sex partners and laws that admonished masturbation were for safeguarding and promoting procreation. Children in biblical times were needed to increase the population to ensure survival of the small tribes and to serve as laborers on farms. Semen was needed to produce children, not be wasted.

The state cannot force churches to perform same-sex marriage, or any other marriage for that matter. Churches often will refuse to perform a marriage for someone who is not in their membership or have a close relative who is. There are churches that will not perform marriages for someone who has been divorced. Many churches will not marry couples who are just church shopping for a great background for their wedding pictures.

I fully support ministers and congregations refusing to perform same-sex marriages. This is a matter of their personal creed, dogma, and/or interpretation of scripture. In the same context, I fully support ministers and congregations performing same sex-marriages.

What I don't support is someone forcing their beliefs on other people. I don't support zealots wanting to write their narrow views of scripture into legislation. This legislation might deny others their chances for happiness and lifetime companionship and more importantly, their basic civil rights. Quoting retired Episcopal Bishop of New Hampshire Gene Robinson writing in *God Believes in Love: Straight Talk about Gay Marriage*, "We don't live in a theocracy where some one understanding of religion and faith dictates what the State will and will not do." (*God Believes in Love: Straight Talk about Gay Marriage*, Gene Robinson, Alfred A. Knopf, NY, 2012, p. 149)

In his scholarly book, *Finally Out*, Dr. Loren Olson, M.D., a Des Moines psychiatrist, stated, "The position of right wing Christianity and of most fundamentalist religions is that everyone is essentially heterosexual and that there is no such thing as homosexual orientation. Homosexuality is seen as a 'lifestyle,' as if it were a choice between living in the city or at the beach. Homosexual feelings and homosexual behavior are seen as equally sinful...When debating the morality of homosexuality, religious conservatives isolate and lift up biblical verses as 'proof texts' to prove that homosexuality is an abomination. Many in the gay community think of these as 'the clobber passages.'" (Loren A. Olson, M.D., *Finally Out: Letting Go of Living Straight*, inGroup Press, 2011, Chicago, p. 40)

I am repulsed by using marriage equality as an emotional rally cry to get people elected to office in order to foster the adoption of an extreme political agenda. Using religion as a political whip is abhorrent. This unethical manipulation by false prophets is simply unacceptable.

Interfaith Alliance of Iowa's excellent brochure "Marriage Equality: Myths and Realities" points out there is not a single belief among faith organizations regarding marriage equality. Some faiths are uncomfortable with homosexuality but many support civil marriage because they believe no one religious group should dictate public policy.

Opponents to marriage equality want to impose their interpretation of the Bible on others. It is used an avenue to get their own extreme agendas into the political arena. Religion is an emotional area which can easily mobilize political muscle. Changing that emotion is difficult if not impossible.

Three-fourths of American Catholics support civil marriage equality as do 81% of adults in the United States under 30. Cardinal Dolan is one of the Catholic Church's outspoken homophobes, supporting the Catholic Church's anti-gay teachings. Dolan stated in an interview on ABC TV (May 31, 2013) "The Week with George Stephanopoulos" that gays and lesbian Catholics feel unwelcomed in the church. He went on to say, "Gays are entitled to friendship. But we also know that God has told us that the way to happiness, that — especially when it comes to sexual love — that is intended only for a man and woman in marriage, where children can come about naturally...We have to do better to see that our defense of marriage is not an attack on gay people." It has been stated that 60% of Catholics say the church is out of touch with views of American Catholics.

The Catholic teachings are that homosexual sexual acts are contrary to natural law, intrinsically immoral and therefore never permissible, while homosexual desires are intrinsically disordered but not in themselves sinful.

Pope Francis' predecessor, Pope Benedict XVI, signed a document in 2005 that said men who had deep-rooted homosexual tendencies should not be priests. Pope Francis was much more conciliatory saying gay clergymen should be forgiven and their sins forgotten. On July 29, 2013 Pope Francis stated, "If someone is gay, who searches for the Lord and has goodwill, who am I to judge?" However, his comments did not signal any change in church policy. Catholic teaching still holds that homosexual acts are "intrinsically disordered."

Confusion was created by those professing to be speaking for God and the manner in which they were delivering God's message. I share the following e-mailer's sentiments.

"I am concerned about the strong hate speeches being made by people who claim to be preachers and God's representatives."

———◆———

McCoy: Somerset Maugham summoned it up this way, "The devil could quote scriptures to his purposes." (*Human Bondage*, W. Somerset Maugham, International Collectors Library /American Headquarters, Garden City, NY @ 1915, 1936, Doubleday & Co., Inc., p. 19)

———◆———

McCoy: An e-mail brings in Mark Twain.

"Mark Twain said, 'It t'aint what you don't know that gets you into trouble. It's what you know for sure to be true but t'aint so.'"

———◆———

"My elation and pride last Friday turned to dread today when I read accounts of Chuck Hurley and his minions from the Iowa Family Policy Center (a made-up, no-meaning name if I ever heard one) trying to strong-arm Governor Culver and the Iowa Legislature into calling a special session just to get the process moving to take away the rights of Iowans that the Iowa Supreme Court just (and justly) affirmed.

I've never understood what exactly it is the Iowa Family Policy Center (*now under the Family Leader*) and their followers hate about gay men and lesbians so much. Has anyone been able to get them off their talking points long enough to get a real answer? If their answer comes from the Bible, why are they not doing the whole job and stoning us to death? If marriage is worth protecting so much, why are they not putting their energy into stopping divorce?"

McCoy: Agendas of hate are seldom sustainable. I want to be a senator that ensures equal liberties for all. A senator who ends discrimination based on one's sexual orientation and who stops bullying in our society. I want to be a senator that brings people together on common ground to broaden our understanding and tolerance of the differences among us. And yes, to celebrate those differences.

McCoy: Hundreds of e-mails citing a religious supported view were sent to all legislators. Writers from both sides of the issue used the same scriptures to support their views.

"SAD SAD DAY IN AMERICA WHEN A MAN AND A WOMEN (sic) GET THEIR RIGHTS TAKEN AWAY BY YOU AND THE FEW!!!!!!!!!!!! Have you dismissed what the Bible says about marriage because you don't think it squares with your own view? If so, think carefully about what you are doing. Do you have the right to veto God's desires? Does it make any sense at all to ignore the counsel of the one who designed marriage? If you have a problem, don't go buy a book that talks about the psychology of marriage...read the Bible! Have you dismissed the teaching about marriage as mere cultural accommodation?"

———

"What happened to GOD, Senator McCoy? God created Adam and Eve not Adam and STEVE. You will have to be accountable to GOD for this ONE! Don't call yourself a Christian, because Christians read the Bible. You obviously missed that in your life."

McCoy: Throughout my life as a Christian, my God was a loving God. I currently am a member of Plymouth Congregational Church in Des Moines. Plymouth has been an open and affirming congregation for over twenty years. The church is affiliated with the United Church of Christ. All are welcomed at Plymouth, regardless who they are or where they are on life's journey. Senior Minister David Ruhe was given a thunderous celebratory standing ovation by 600 congregants upon completing his sermon celebrating Plymouth's twenty year anniversary of being an open and affirming congregation. Ruhe challenged congregants to continue to follow Christ's example of lovingly embracing those pushed to the margins of society.

In September 2014, Plymouth completed a $1.7M renovation of their sanctuary. The first wedding in that beautifully renovated sacred place will be between two women who have been together for 21 years.

———

"We stand with thousands of same-sex couples, affirming their freedom to marry the person they love." (United Church of Christ).

———

"This whole move from the so called 'religious' right is not only offensive, but horrifying. Civil rights given to gays who wish to marry will not in any way affect their personal lives, or be an attempt to sway their personal beliefs. They don't have any argument that is valid to say that any two people of consenting age cannot marry, nor would they have the right in any state in this nation to deny any citizen equal rights."

McCoy: We have made progress. But despite that progress, we've also been a whipping post to the right-wingers and the self-proclaimed Christians. They have come forward stating that they know what's best for us, that we will somehow endanger their marriages if we get married. They spread more lies, perpetuate more hatred and more bigotry than any group I know.

"PLEASE FIGHT AGAINST THIS EVIL PERVERSION CALLED GAY MARRIAGE HERE IN IOWA. IT WILL BE THE RUINATION OF MANY FAMILIES, OF OUR STATE, OUR NATION AND OUR WORLD. PLEASE SAY 'NO' TO THIS EVIL DRIVEN WARFARE CALLED SAME SEX MARRIAGE. NO ONE WILL BENEFIT FROM IT EXCEPT SATAN HIMSELF. DO NOT FALL FOR HIS LIES AND DECEIT. IT IS APPARENT MANY OF YOU HAVE, BUT IT'S NOT TOO LATE TO CHANGE. LIFE IS SHORT, ETERNITY IS FOREVER. WHERE DO YOU WANT TO SPEND YOURS????

THE SUPREME COURT BROKE THE LAW AS FAR AS I'M CONCERNED. THEY WILL BE PUNISHED DEARLY BY OUR DEAR LORD. THE SALVATION OF THE PEOPLE OF THIS STATE, THE STATE ITSELF AND OUR ONCE GREAT NATION LIES IN YOUR HANDS AND YOU WILL BE HELD ACCOUNTABLE FOR HUNDREDS OF THOUSANDS OF SOULS. PLEASE SAY 'NO' TO SAME SEX MARRIAGE. THIS I BEG OF YOU."

McCoy: The above e-mail stands in stark contrast to Matt Mardis-LeCroy's comments upon receiving the "Protecting Faith and Freedom Award" from the Interfaith Alliance of Iowa (May 21, 2012). Mardis-LeCroy, Senior Minister Elect,

Plymouth Congregation Church, Des Moines, Iowa, stated: "Thank you for your commitment to our shared vision of what the State of Iowa that can be, what the state that Iowa must be: a place where welcome is extended and dignity affirmed for every last person; a place where our different faith traditions are not divided by ignorance and hostility but united in doing good; a place where religion has a positive and healing role to play in our public life."

McCoy — John B. Harper, retired English professor at The University of Iowa and an Episcopal priest wrote the following on his Facebook page (August 13, 2013): "I'm sick and tired of 'Christian' churches driving young people to commit suicide. I'm weary of having to counsel parents to run away from their churches in order to save their families and the lives of their children. Jesus must be furious!"

It is estimated that one-third of teenage suicides are committed by LGBT youth.

"Gay rights concerning marriage is wrong. Take a stand for righteousness according to the Word of God. Many are with you and praying for you to do that which is right and within your power, which was given to you by the people and God."

McCoy: A letter came from a pastor in eastern Iowa.

"As you are well aware, the decision 'opinion' by the court has been insulting to Iowans across the state. To repeal the law and consider it unconstitutional, after our legislature had worked to defend marriage through the Defense of Marriage Act, was extremely arrogant. No matter how often it's said through media channels, homo sex is not an immutable gene someone is born with. It is not a normative. Both the medical field and scientific community continue to show study after study that refutes this lie. I implore you, as an honorable servant of the people of Iowa, not to allow the heartland of our nation to become the stimulus of homosexual marriage across America.

For at least the last two thousand years, civilized people have understood the nature of homosexuality and the social, physical and emotional problems involved. Every great society has condemned the sexual behavior of homosexuality.

History has already warned us. In his 1979 book *Our Dance Has Turned To Death*, sociologist Carl Wilson outlined the dangers facing traditional marriage and the family in our increasingly sexual culture. He writes, 'History reveals that nations decline and eventually die when sexual immorality becomes unrestrained and normative! If the traditional family of one man and one woman is discarded in favor of group sex, homo sex, infidelity and unrestrained sexual hedonism, cultural norms will not survive.'

Russian sociologist Pitirum Sorokin wrote *The American Sex Revolution* in which he warned that America was in the process of committing 'voluntary suicide' through unrestrained sexual indulgence.

Sexual promiscuity and the loss of respect for the sanctity of marriage lead inevitably to a cultural decline and sadly eventual collapse. We need your courageous leadership and fearless stand against same-sex marriage."

McCoy: Words from A Franciscan Benediction comes to mind:

May God bless us with discomfort at easy answers, half-truths, and superficial relationships, so that we may live deep within our hearts.

May God bless us with anger at injustice, oppression, and exploitation of people, so that we may work for justice, freedom and peace.

And may God bless us with enough foolishness to believe that we can make a difference in this world, so that we can do what others claim cannot be done.

McCoy: Not all writers felt the economic well-being of the state would be improved through marriage equality.

"As a native born Iowan I am outraged by the decision of our Supreme Court overturning the ban on gay marriage. Will you allow our future to be decimated by such abhorrent behavior? If no action is taken, we will encourage our friends to move with us to neighboring states that will not condone such immoral behavior, and we will conduct all our business in neighboring states."

"I am disappointed that our state has stooped so low as to turn their back on God by allowing such a thing that is an abomination to God!!! Of course you realize I'm speaking of homosexual marriage. The people were not even allowed a vote in this ugly decision. No matter what your feelings may be in this matter, I humbly request that you do everything in your power to give the people a chance to vote on this issue."

"I believe the majority of people in the state of Iowa are Christians. The decision by the Iowa Supreme Court to legalize same sex marriage is a disgrace and out of touch with what Christians believe is morally in line with the word of God. If you don't do something to counter what the Supreme Court has done, I will no longer believe that your values represent our values and I will make sure those voters I know don't vote for any of you."

McCoy: I, too, am a Christian. As such, I recognize and accept that huge differences exist among those of the Christian faith as you can see from the following excerpt from a Methodist newsletter:

"Methodist rules once prevented women from ordained ministry, tolerated slavery and established separate 'Jurisdictions' for African-American churches. Church rules and biblical interpretation of these issues changed because of compassion and new understanding. We believe this is currently happening on the issue of homosexuality. While some people point to a few sections of the Bible to condemn homosexuality, we recognize the emphasis throughout the Scriptures on love and inclusion. There is no prohibition of homosexuality in the Ten Commandments... Nor did Jesus mention homosexuality in any of the Gospels." (THE/REPORTER, January/February, 2014, p. 5, Administrative Board of Grace United Methodist Church, Des Moines, IA)

"Just read the Bible and you will see that God does not condone same sex marriage! Thank you!"

McCoy: I do read the Bible. I believe the words in the Bible to be eternal but over time its meaning has evolved.

"The Bible states in Lev. 18:22 'Thou shall not lie with mankind as with womankind it is abomination.'"

McCoy: Well then I assume you also believe Leviticus 15:19 which states that women are unclean during their menstrual cycle. Anyone who touches them or sits or lies where they have sat or laid is also unclean. Literal interpretation of this would probably offend most of today's women. From where you are coming, as an apparent fundamentalist, I wonder how do you justify picking and choosing from the Bible what you believe?

Jesus never spoke of marriage equality. Yet, there are preachers, activists, and would-be politicians who claim to speak for God with their spiteful speeches against marriage equality. I can't believe that God or Jesus would choose people like this to be their spokesperson. Nor can I believe that some new translations of the Bible are actually changing text to include the word "homosexuality."

"I would simply but strongly urge that in your decision making processes that you take into consideration whom the outcome of your decision will please, God or man. You are a child of the Most High God, your name is written on the palm of His hand. He knows you by name and He desperately loves you. There is not a person you are representing here on this earth that adores you the way God does nor has sacrificed for you the way He has. Line up your opinion with God not man and let God deal with His beloved children. My intent is to help settle any self-conflict you may be having with this matter but my hope is that you take this advise into all future decision making to keep you in peace. Because as you know there is coming a day when we shall all stand before Him and give an account of our lives and I'm sure you, like me, want to hear the words 'well done good and faithful servant, well done.' Let's represent Him well together."

"The Iowa Supreme Court decided to desecrate the sanctity of marriage and our constitution by taking matters into their own hands in saying a ban on same-sex marriage was unconstitutional. I am not a rabble-rouser, or a pessimist, but I am also not one whose conscience is able to stand on the sidelines when it comes to standing up for what I know is right. Some may call me a hater, evil, discriminatory, etc. Unfortunately, it is nothing I haven't heard before. I and many others are willing to put up with this if it means protecting the sacred institution of the family."

McCoy: Although it is flattering to have been addressed as "Statesman" that's all I might agree with in the following e-mail.

"Dear Statesman McCoy: The very decision that the seven Iowa Supreme Court Justices made goes AGAINST the Word of the Creator. When one begins to fear the LORD that person begins to have wisdom."

McCoy: Over the top rhetoric created drama.

"I find all this talk of homosexual marriage both morally wrong and personally offensive. Homosexuality is socially destructive, contrary to nature and, more importantly, contrary to the law of God. It is wrong in every way, and decent people should not have to hide that fact. To pretend that evil has become good does not change the fact or render the evil any less wicked. You have the capability of stopping this! If you don't — you will be showing that money is more important than your morals and that you have sold your soul to rich homosexual activists. I hope not, but from what I can tell, you don't seem to have the guts it takes to do what's right for the people of this state!"

McCoy: Writers were also objective, understanding a broader view that extended beyond their own religious beliefs.

"We believe in equal rights for all citizens. We are not gay; our religious beliefs do not approve of gay marriage. Neither, however, do our religious beliefs approve of spreading false rumors, false information and false witness against our neighbors. Many untruths about the reasons why the Marriage Law was found to be unconstitutional are being spread by so-called Christian leaders and their followers. We hope that you will also live up to the vows you took when you became an elected official and also find it one of your duties to your electorate to TRUTHFULLY explain why and how this ruling occurred. Even though we are not a part of this minority group, we believe that they are entitled to equal treatment, as both the state of Iowa and the U.S. Constitution guarantee. If the majority of our citizens were homosexuals, we would certainly not want a law that specified that the only recognized form of marriage had to be between two men or between two women. Neither option is just or equal or should be the law."

McCoy: Two ministers signed the following e-mail.

"Please allow our constitution to remain unchanged in its ability to provide equal treatment for all. If one exception is made, it will be easier to make a second and then a third, etc. Equal treatment regarding civil marriage changes NOTHING for anyone who isn't gay and harms NO ONE. The various religious groups who oppose same sex marriage can continue to promise an eternity in Hell to gays and maybe they'll be right. They can also continue to work to 'save those heathens' from that damnation. Civil law and religious law should remain separate."

"I have a suggestion. Why don't you change the law to read: 'Marriage is between an adult man and an adult woman according to God's laws. Civil Unions are between same sex adults or atheists according to civil laws. Both shall have the same legal rights according to state's laws.' I think this would be a fair compromise."

McCoy: Although I share your sentiments on seeking common ground, the term 'civil union' does not elevate such relationships to the level of "marriage" and the love, commitments, respect, and legal benefits that accompany it. The two are not equal.

McCoy: Many parents continue to be proud of and support their gay off-spring in spite of positions their churches may have taken.

"Please keep in mind that bigotry, inequality, and discrimination not to mention all types of torture, murder and horrific atrocities have occurred in the name of religion. And historically, fear out of ignorance, unfamiliarity or misunderstanding has been the basis for the bigotry and discrimination. PLEASE, do not let Iowa continue to practice inequality and discrimination out of fear and ignorance. I was raised and married in the Baptist Church. We are proud parents of a gay child."

McCoy — from Tennessee came this protest:

"It has come to my attention there is an issue in your state concerning marriage. The issue is that the law which upholds marriage as between one man and one woman may be set aside at the whim of the judges trying to change what has been established. They are trying to replace traditional marriage with recognition of licensed homosexual and lesbian marriages.

Our country is in one of the most vulnerable positions it has ever been in and the agenda of the American Civil Liberties Union (ACLU), the Gay Rights movement, and all associated and like groups — has been a proponent of undermining the values and morals of our once mighty, ethical and moral country.

Sexual preference is a personal issue, but this country was founded on Christian morals, and those principles do NOT condone gay marriage as part of the law of the land. The majority of the people in this country DO NOT WANT THESE RULES TO BE CHANGED. Help protect us and our children." (Tennessee)

McCoy: Malcolm Boyd is a well known Episcopal priest who happens to be gay. Boyd is the author of *Gay Priest: An Inner Journey*. His life partner is Mark Thompson. The following is an excerpt from an interview with Boyd found in Mark Thompson's anthology *Gay Soul: Finding the Heart of Gay Spirit and Nature with Sixteen Writers, Healers, Teachers, and Visionaries*. (Harper, San Francisco, A Division of Harper Collins Publishers, 1994)

"**Mark Thompson:** You've asked, is Jesus gay? Don't you mean *was*?

Malcolm Boyd: I have no theory about the historical Jesus. But in Christ I find many gay qualities: vulnerability, sensitivity, someone who emptied himself of power, who lived as a gentle but strong person. He also broke many social taboos and found sterling qualities in a number of people who were despised by the society they lived in. He is very much a gay archetype in my understanding of what being gay means.

Thompson: What is it about the church that attracts so many gay men?

Boyd: Where were gays ever going to go in the past but the military or the church? And the church dealt in mystery, beauty, music, and ritual. These are things that speak to gay men.

Thompson: You are one of very few gay men with such a high profile to have dared to come out, even in a place as liberal as the Episcopal Church. What is the price of staying closeted in the church?

Boyd: I have never seen such bitterness, vindictiveness, and cruelty as I have on the part of closeted gay priests. These are people who have chosen to live a lie and have paid a high price — a price of happiness and freedom. What do they get back? A certain prestige, which they guard with their life."

Boyd observed: "Reading these words I cannot help but think of those within the clerical caste of the Roman Catholic Church working so hard to deny civil marriage rights to gay couples. How much of their vindictive and cruel campaign is fueled by their loathing of themselves as gay men? I've long maintained that the most dangerous and rabid opponents of gay people and gay rights are closeted gay people. And when such closet cases are in positions of secular or religious power, the potential for anti-Gospel rhetoric and behavior, for lies and fear-mongering, and thus pain and harm to individuals, couples, families, society and the church, is very great. We must never hesitate to challenge such people and the vindictive and cruel campaigns they devise and direct."

McCoy: Do I think Jesus was gay? No, probably not. But that begs the question, "What difference would it make?" The excerpt from the interview between Boyd and Thompson was included to bring to the forefront that many stereotypes of gay qualities — negative, unmanly stereotypes — hurled at gay men can be found in Boyd's description of Jesus. This is not meant to be insensitive nor offensive. I too follow the Lord. I hope the inclusion of this clip will expand awareness of the narrowness and dangers of stereotyping.

——————

McCoy: Bishop Julius C. Trimbe, Iowa Annual Conference of the United Methodist Church, Des Moines, issued a statement on the Iowa Supreme Court Decision.

"I have decided not to accept an invitation from Catholic Bishops of Iowa and other religious leaders in condemning the Iowa Supreme Court. I strongly believe the Iowa Supreme Court acted with judicial integrity in its determination that 'civil' marriage must be judged under constitutional standards of equal protections and not under religious doctrines or religious views of individuals." **(Trimbe's entire statement can be found in Appendix A, page 180.)**

McCoy — One of my constituents who is in a committed same-sex relationship, writes:

"Catholic priests choose not to marry people who are not Catholic. Pastors of other denominations often through counseling decide that they are unable to marry a couple based on what they see. Choosing to perform this wonderful ceremony of love and grace is still their choice. No one is taking that away.

I ask you to remember that there is a separation of church and state because things have been confused in the past. Interracial marriage was also a religious topic many years ago and you know how wrong that was. Please let my family live with the rights and obligations that other families live with. Let us live in freedom and love, not fear and frustration."

"I oppose gay marriage. It's wrong. You got a problem with that? Take it up with God."

McCoy: A citizen from Louisiana chimed in on the controversy. The writer of the e-mail below sent it to all the senators and representatives. That took considerable time to compile and type the 150 addresses to the legislators reflecting the writer's strong commitment.

"In the beginning God didn't create Adam and Adam. He created Adam and Eve. Please do not condemn the entire country, because you allowed this evil into our society. Think of your children and how you'd like them to be raised. Please get down on your knees and pray that God will change the hearts of those trying to pass gay marriage. Instead live by God's standards and watch Him do a mighty work in your state!!!!! I don't even live in Iowa, but I am so burdened with the way our society thinks that just because one or two may believe a certain way, that it doesn't mean that we believe and live like the devil." (Louisiana)

———

"People that use that tired old catch-phrase of 'God didn't make Adam and Steve!' don't seem to realize that actually, God DID make Adam and Steve. If not God, who?"

———

"The highest court of Iowa sins. In gratitude to the LORD God Yahweh, ruler of the Universe and sovereign over those who name Him as king, and purest motivator of their hearts, we of the state of Iowa are aghast at this treatment today of Him by the Supreme Court of Iowa and call for their individual hearts to be torn in repentance for this evil decision. May our hearts and mouths cry out unto Him for forgiveness for this evil ruling as the justices of the Iowa Supreme Court tempt the wrath of God upon the people of Iowa. Marriage is a holy union between one man and one woman necessitated for sanction of physical union by Almighty God. May the LORD inflict His justice for this ruling down upon their own heads and all who argued and labored in favor of the abomination and spare the people of Iowa who oppose this defiance of God."

McCoy: This is so different than the message of a loving God that is preached in my church. "Let your light shine. Even while others try to snuff it out...It takes courage to seize the life that God gives us...How many of us have struggled to define ourselves against the expectations of our communities, even our churches, or families?...Everyone seems to know what I need better than I do?...It's awesome to be in the presence of someone who just is who she is, without apology or explanation...Let it shine! Gay or straight or bisexual. Let it shine!" (Cameron Barr, Associate Minister, Plymouth Congregational Church, Des Moines, *Sermon,* February 9, 2014)

"We have many more issues to deal with than those raised by an embittered, isolated minority of Christian conservatives who are as out of touch with the New Testament as they are with the Old. What's being offered by this crowd is theocracy, which I firmly reject and believe is not what Jesus asked us to do."

"We all have friends or family members who we know in our soul did not 'choose' a life of persecution. The suicide rate for gays tells the true story of self-hatred our outdated judgments impose upon our gay friends. Our nation has come so far by electing a man of color to the presidency, overcoming years of codified discrimination. Please don't advocate a new kind of state-mandated discrimination by amending our constitution."

"There is no reason beyond fear and religious narrow-mindedness to strip same-sex couples of the right to marry. It will be a shameful day if Iowans take away this right."

"I am appalled and outraged by the audacity you have to destroy marriage. Marriage is ordained of God from the beginning of time in the Garden of Eden.

<u>You have offended me, my Lord, my God; You have insulted the very Word of God.</u>

This is an insult to the Christian Believers, the Jewish Community, & possibly Muslims. I encourage you to REVERSE this unrighteous decision. Those who agree with this proposal need to repent and be restored unto the Lord of Heaven.

Procreation occurs between a man and woman, so that the earth may be filled with the Glory of God. A reflection of God's purity, not a reflection of filth & rebellion.

God destroyed the cities of Sodom & Gomorrah because of their filthy behaviors.

Please do all you can to overturn this Abomination before God, I pray you will choose the correct response to this situation.

NOTE — God Loves Each Of Us — but hates sinful behavior, His desire for each of us is to walk in Purity & Holiness, Obeying His Holy Word. Let us choose His Way, not our way. Sometimes our way can lead to a temporary spiritual death, sometimes even eternal death. Let us ask forgiveness for our sins. We don't give alcoholics special rights, addicts' special rights, smokers' special rights."

—————

Matt: Comments from Resolution 3-05A enacted in the 2004 Convention of The Lutheran Church — Missouri Synod (LCMS), condemnation of same-sex marriage follows. (A copy that has been edited for length may be found in Appendix B, page 181.)

WHEREAS, 'That the Synod recognize homophile behavior as intrinsically sinful"

WHEREAS, Homosexual behavior is prohibited in the Old and New Testaments

WHEREAS, For our Synod to be silent, especially in the present context, could be viewed as acceptance of the homosexual lifestyle; therefore be it

Resolved, That the Synod urge its members to give a public witness from Scripture against the social acceptance and legal recognition of homosexual 'marriage';"

—————

Matt: The following heartfelt e-mail was received from a Roman Catholic priest.

"I must admit I am saddened by the decision today to allow same-sex marriages. The people of Iowa were not given a chance to vote on this matter. It was handed down to them. To me, this is inching toward despotism. This social engineering by the state to re-define marriage will end up harming children and society as a whole. How, you might say? Children are hard-wired to be raised by a mother and father. The state has had a legitimate interest in favoring such traditional marriages as a way of investing in the future of society by providing for the human flourishing of future generations. We are also aware in the face of increasing individualism and relativism, the state has retreated from promoting these interests either through no-fault divorce or Roe vs. Wade. Yet, marriage is not the invention of the state, but it came from God. It is an age-old institution that neither you nor I have the authority or right to change. Same-sex marriage holds that anyone can create their own reality. Truth then becomes determined by one's own will, not natural law. Truth is not contrived, invented, or made-up. To defend marriage as monogamous union between one man and one woman is not bigotry, homophobic, or intolerance as many opponents of same-sex marriage use to silence or marginalize those who support traditional marriages. I am heartened by the Bishops of Iowa who have stood up for the truth on this issue in the face of pressure and persecution!

They are fighting hard against the dictatorship of relativism!

Thanks for listening. I will keep you in my prayers on a daily basis. God's Blessing and Peace!"

McCoy: Sen. Majority Leader Mike Gronstal received the following e-mail which he shared with our caucus.

"…What homosexuals really want is acceptance of their perverse behavior before a righteous Creator. I long for a Creator ordained leader who would bring a righteousness back into the public arena within America, like Moses and Elijah, and put an end to the in-your-face rebellion...Glad to see this legislative leadership going home."

———————

McCoy: The following e-mail came from a very controversial constituent. As you will discern, this writer has very strong views which are often quoted by the media. The person is not without a following on this as well as other "biblical based" issues such as abortion.

"You've made a dramatic journey from traditional pro-life Catholic to leader of Iowa's movement to the legal recognition of homosexual marriage. I would love to understand that journey and share it with the public."

McCoy — *my response was:*

Thanks for your e-mail. There is no question that I have continued to grow and change as a person. At the basis of that change, what has remained, is an inherent sense of "fairness" and respect for all individuals regardless of their sexual orientation.

What you are asking me about is also deeply personal and intimate with respect to my coming to terms about my own sexuality. Somehow, I don't feel the format you suggest to sharing this is appropriate.

He replied: "Thanks for your response. I didn't have in mind prying into your personal sexuality, which I think would be more uncomfortable for me than for you. My real curiosity is about your journey from a relatively Christian faith wherein acts are right and wrong because some give us genuine satisfaction and others deceive us with pseudo satisfaction, and we trust God's identification of which is which — to more of a humanistic faith in which God is perceived as not necessarily meaning precisely what the Bible says He means, so we ought to extend fairness equally to biblical wrong as to biblical right.

That characterization of your journey is of course only my best guess. I would like to understand better. For example, have you felt betrayed in some way by the teaching you lived by before?"

McCoy: *End of correspondence.*

———————

"Those citizens who feel the majority's religious view ought to prevail for all of society may wish to consider that many Europeans who made their way to this continent did so to escape the oppression of the religious majorities in Europe. These fringe groups were squeezed out of their native lands and were eager to escape the endless religious wars. This persecution led to a radically new idea in the history of the world, the separation of church and state.

It would also be good to remember that not all the founding fathers were orthodox Christians. Many were deists. Thomas Jefferson edited his own version of the New Testament to take out all the parts he found objectionable. Alexander Hamilton, author of that wonderful quote about God's law trumping all human law, no doubt thought he was on God's side — as in his support for a strong central government and implied powers, creating national debt as good fiscal policy, and his affair with Maria Reynolds (who pushed him from public life). Oh, and his fatal duel with Vice President Burr. Is this someone we want to quote about God's will?

It has often been said that freedom of religion means freedom from other people's religion. It ought to be obvious by now that religious people often find each other's religions odious. Religious ideas will always vary as they always have. That is why we have congregations and denominations. Can we please remember our own history and stop trying to impose our personal religious views onto our secular laws and governance?"

———————

McCoy: The Iowa Catholic Conference submitted a Statement on an Iowa Constitutional Amendment regarding Marriage (April 2009) that was authorized by Republican Iowa State Senator Jerry Behn for distribution to the desks of all Iowa senators. Excerpts follow. (The full statement can be found in Appendix C, page 182.)

"Marriage is a basic human and social institution. Though it is regulated by civil laws and church laws, it did not originate from either the church or state, but from God. Therefore, neither church nor state can alter the basic meaning and structure of marriage.

...it is important to work towards the passage of an amendment to Iowa's Constitution which would define marriage as being between one man and one woman.

We are convinced that the passage of this amendment is important for the following reasons.

First, Marriage between a man and a woman is good from the perspectives of both natural law and our Catholic faith...

Secondly, Children who are raised by a married father and mother have more positive outcomes, including behavioral and educational accomplishments.

Thirdly, Cohabitation and divorce laws have already contributed to a weakening of marriage. . .

Fourthly, Social engineering by judges or legislatures adds to the confusion about the good that marriage offers to society, and weakens the critical relationship between marriage and parenting.

Therefore, we call on Catholics to support the need for a constitutional amendment."

Matt: The following letter was authorized for distribution to all senators by Senator Merlin Bartz, Republican from northwestern Iowa. In the letter he unsuccessfully attempted to give county recorders the authority to deny granting marriage licenses to same-gender couples if it was against their faith beliefs. Bartz's effort following the court's ruling was the first test at sabotaging the effort to comply with the law. Bartz's Senatorial district was redistricted. In his next election he lost to a Democrat. The problem with Bartz's political grandstanding was its potential harmful impact on people and families.

Everyday America
Joint Statement on Constitutional 'Marriage' Crisis
April 13, 2009

Des Moines — The following organizations are calling for the Iowa Legislature to resolve the inherent conflict between Iowa Code 595.2 which still states 'only marriage between a male and a female is valid' and the court ordered issuance of same-sex marriage licenses. These groups believe this is an issue that can only be resolved through the normal legislative process. Further, they assert that if a legislative solution is not found, Governor Culver must issue an executive order preventing any same-sex marriage licenses from being issued until the conflict is resolved.

Signed by,

Everyday America
Iowa Family Center ACTION
Concerned Women for America
Eagle Forum of Iowa
Iowa Christian Alliance
Iowa Baptists for Biblical Values
Network of Iowa Christian Home Educators

McCoy: Governor Culver could not legally have done what Bartz and these signers ordered him to do. Understanding

the law and following the law are separate issues from just interpreting the law according to what you wish it meant.

———————

McCoy: Biblical verses were twisted to support positions against marriage equality. Those doing so view their interpretation of the Bible as absolute. All other interpretations by other Christians and churches are considered to be wrong. What's really wrong is their assumption they are right. Interfaith Alliance of Iowa took a strong and courageous stand against such dogma.

Interfaith Alliance of Iowa is a statewide, non-partisan organization working to protect both faith and freedom in Iowa. It encourages committed community activism to challenge extremism and defend the civil rights of Iowans. They empower Iowans to become actively and effectively involved in the political process as a progressive voice of faith and goodwill.

Interfaith Alliance of Iowa called upon religious leaders in Iowa to come together in support of marriage equality and to challenge dogma. In their letter to all Iowa state senators and representatives, signers stated their opposition to the use of the Bible to deny equal protection and responsibility under the law for gay and lesbian couples. They recognized the state does not require clergy who disagree with same-gender marriage to officiate ceremonies of gay and lesbian couples. The letter dated February 16, 2010, was signed by 164 clergy from many faiths in churches across Iowa, in support of the state upholding the rights of its citizens. (Full text of the letter and signatures may be found in Appendix D, page 184.)

McCoy: Plymouth Congregational Church describes itself as a "progressive congregation" that numbers more than 3,000 members. Its Board of Christian Social Action developed a resolution which later was approved by its Church Council speaking for the entire church. I authorized copies of their "Marriage Equality Policy" to be distributed to the desks of all Iowa state senators. Similar approval was given by State Representative Jo Oldson for distribution in the Iowa House of Representatives. It immediately created quite a stir among conservative senators who quickly scurried around to develop their own statement expressing opposition to marriage equality. They distributed it the following day. Plymouth's statement came at the height of the marriage equality controversy when leaders of many — most? — congregations shied away from taking positions of support to avoid what could be a divisive issue for their congregations. (The statement may be found in its entirety in Appendix E, page 190.) The resolution proclaimed:

"THEREFORE LET IT BE RESOLVED, that Plymouth Congregational Church of the United Church of Christ affirms equal access to the basic rights, institutional protections and quality of life conferred by the recognition of marriage; and

LET IT BE FURTHER RESOLVED, that the officers, ministers and members of Plymouth Congregational Church of the United Church of Christ are called upon to communicate this resolution to appropriate local, state and national legislators, urging them to support equal marriage rights for couples regardless of gender.

The Church Council
Plymouth Congregational Church of the United Church of Christ
4126 Ingersoll Avenue
Des Moines, Iowa 50312

January 26, 2010"

McCoy: On April 14, 2013 I was a guest on a local news spot "Three Minutes in the Chair" with T.V. Channel 13's Dan Winters.

Winters: McCoy has never shied away from sharing his beliefs...Would you be opposed to the legislature getting rid of the word "marriage" and leaving that word up to churches where it began?

McCoy: I would not be opposed to that, ultimately civil unions are just that — civil unions.

Winters: You want a level plane.

McCoy: Yes, I don't want one elevated over another I have always said if we're going to have marriage, let's have marriage for all. If we're going to have civil unions, let's have civil unions for all. What the churches do with it inside their own institutions is up to them. And, we should have absolutely no interference.

Winters: Why not sponsor a bill that would do this and end all of this fighting?

McCoy: Well frankly, the religious clergy have opposed that.

Winters: You're saying the clergy wants to give the power over marriage to the government?

McCoy: Yes. They see it as a right of the government to convey marriage.

Winters: But if it were up to you, you'd give power of marriage back to churches?

McCoy: Absolutely. I would do civil unions for all. But we leave the sacrament of marriage up to the churches.

McCoy: We have a lot of work to do to separate people from their stereotypic thinking of gays as a sub-class of humans to accepting them as equals. With this acceptance we will stop denying them the same privileges, rights, and yes, marriage equality that has given our lives such deep meaning.

"Perverse lifestyle? What is perverse are those who think homosexuality is a choice, a lifestyle, or that it can be cured by some sort of voodoo therapy or even religion?"

————

McCoy: The severity of some of the comments from adults who might be parents more than concerned me. I feared this same hurtful language was likely to be used in their homes when talk turns to gays, gay marriage, homosexuals, etc. Their children would be subject to these torrents of hate. Should one of them happen to be gay, the poor kid would be driven deeper into the closet with its accompanying self-loathing. Tragically, we are aware this despair has led to suicide.

Conservatives whine about government intruding in their lives and family lives, yet they have no difficulty in discriminating against same-gender couples seeking marriage equality or intruding into their bedrooms.

Being gay does not mean being incapable of love or not wanting to have the security of a long-term committed relationship. I would think happily married hetero couples would get this. With the current high divorce rate at 40% (Public News Services — TN March 2013) in the United States for traditional marriages, gays have been asked why they'd want to get married. Britney Speers' marriage lasted 55 hours while in comparison Kim Kardashian's first marriage was long term before she filed for divorce 72 days after her lavish wedding. I think these are the things that threaten "till death do us part."

This rally poster should be reassuring to zealots opposing sex-gender marriage: "Jesus had two dads and he turned out fine."

Chapter 5: Social Media Gone Wild

"Fair minded people throughout the state support equality for all."

Senator Matt McCoy

The long-awaited announcement from the Iowa Supreme Court on marriage equality was to come down on April 3, 2009. I was ready with a carefully prepared press release to celebrate this milepost in the history of civil rights and to assure citizens this was not a passing moment. My press conference was televised and immediately posted on YouTube which got 21,000 hits. (My full speech may be found in Appendix F, page 192.) My speech included the following:

Today is a red letter day for the State of Iowa. All of Iowa's citizens now have equal protection under the law.

Here's why I believe Iowa will not go backwards when it comes to civil rights:

One: Iowa has a long history of civil rights leadership.

- In 1839, the Iowa Supreme Court rejected slavery in a decision that found that a slave named Ralph became free when he stepped on Iowa soil, 26 years before the end of the Civil War decided the issue.
- In 1868, the Iowa Supreme Court ruled that racially segregated "separate but equal" schools had no place in Iowa, 85 years before the U.S. Supreme Court reached the same decision.
- In 1869, Iowa became the first state in the union to admit women to the practice of law.
- In 1873, the Iowa Supreme Court ruled against racial discrimination in public accommodations, 91 years before the U.S. Supreme Court reached the same decision.

Two: Social conservatives have made their case to Iowans and been rejected.

Three: The Iowa Constitution can't be changed quickly.

I believe marriage equality is here to stay, and Iowans will quickly realize that it is no big deal.

———————

McCoy: Social media exploded over the impending Supreme Court's decision. It played a critical role in activating people to defeat the religious opposition. Facebook fans adopted the red equality (=) sign from the Human Rights Campaign as part of an electronic campaign to voice support of marriage equality. At the time of the court hearings it was estimated that approximately 2.5 million Facebook users changed their profile images to a red equals logo (Same-sex marriage in the United States, Wikipedia).

Following my April 3, 2009 press conference comments cited above, there were 401 written blogs. Blogs that followed were not only directed to me but to other bloggers. They covered the full range from being proud to be an Iowan to being convinced we are all headed for damnation. Bloggers tend to be blunt under the cover of anonymity. Be prepared, some blogs are downright vulgar but, read on.

———————

"I hope Senator McCoy never complains about the hot Iowa summers, cause where he's going it's gonna be a HELL of a lot hotter. Try all you want homos, God will still descend upon you in judgment."

———————

"So, Iowa won't go backwards on 'marriage right' probably because their tractors won't go in reverse. So, they'll just make a u-turn on them and return to where the mistake was made and correct it."

"A monumental act of humane decency in a world full of scared and fearful people."

"That's my Senator! Go you!"

"So, what's next? Are we going to allow necrophilia's to marry corpses? How about allowing pedophiles to marry children? No one is born gay."

"Seeing as how Iowa is a leading farming state with a huge # of cattle, this is just another example of the manure produced by the state."

"Hopefully, the state constitution allows for a referendum that can reverse this ill-thought move and bring some sanity back to the state."

"1 Samuel 18: 1-3: And it came to pass when David had made an end of speaking unto Saul, that the soul of Jonathan was knit with the soul of David, and Jonathan loved him as his own soul...And Jonathan and David made a covenant, because he loved him as his own soul. And immediately afterward, Jonathan DISROBED before David.' Gay marriage existed in the Bible!"

McCoy: The following was written to another blogger.

"Spoken like a true Republican — four grammatical errors in a nine word 'sentence'"

"Christians keep your disgusting filth out of my life. I will, as always, GLADLY stay out of yours."

"The church is welcome to teach whatever lies it wishes."

"But you're correct — we should follow biblical principles. You know, stoning to death adulterers, children who don't respect their parents, shellfish eaters, and, of course, those who wear clothing of more than one fabric. Oh, wait, that would be EVERYONE!"

"'Gay marriage impedes on other's religious beliefs.' And how does it do that? Really? I would like someone to explain it to me. Where gay marriage is legal people can still attend church, pray and still believe whatever they want (including that being gay is evil)."

"YOU need to follow ALL of the rules in Leviticus if you're going to use it to fight against gay marriage:

- Don't cut your sideburns.

- Don't touch a woman during her period.

- Don't touch the skin of a dead pig…and-on-and-on and-on."

"If you believe the Bible is absolutely literal in all aspects, then you should follow it completely. LEVITICUS was meant to rule the Israelites of the time, NOT today. By the way, how many times have YOU been married?"

―――――――

"I'm ashamed to be from Iowa."

―――――――

"We need a Republican back in the governor's seat. I'm sorry to be from IOWA right now."

―――――――

"So it will be ok if gays vote on your private love life? Because that is what it comes down to is straight people deciding with whom we can and cannot spend the rest of our lives."

―――――――

"Separation of church and state. Keep the Bible out of the law. This has NOTHING to do with religion. It is CIVIL RIGHTS. If you want to hate people using your religion to do so, fine, but keep it out of my life."

―――――――

"Thank you for what you do, Senator your message is powerful, your message is love, your message is heard."

―――――――

"I used to be gay."

―――――――

"I thought the Boy Scouts hated gay people, so how did you become an Eagle Scout?"

―――――――

"The church can teach whatever it wants to its congregants. The state has no obligation to make its institutions reflect a church's values. Certain churches encourage polygamy, for example, but this doesn't mean that polygamy should be legal. I'm not saying that it should, only that a church's endorsement of it should have no bearing on its legality."

"Have you even READ the Constitution? By definition a Supreme Court ruling cannot be unconstitutional. The Constitution says what the Supreme Court says it says. That is the job of the court, to interpret the Constitution. If the State Supreme Court says Iowa must recognize gay marriage then until that ruling is either overturned by a higher court or a subsequent ruling, or the constitution is amended, the Iowa Constitution recognizes gay marriage. That's how constitutional law works."

"The Constitution explicitly prevents the majority from oppressing the minority. If you want a pure democracy, throw out the constitution; if you want a constitutional democracy, then the constitution will sometimes trump the will of the masses."

"Constitutional amendments have almost always served to increase individual liberty. The only exception was prohibition, and that was clearly a mistake. To pass an amendment that limits personal freedom is contrary to the spirit of the Constitution itself."

"All of Iowa must be proud!! Now if I love two women I can marry them. If I love my dog I can marry her and we're a family. IOWANS voted for this man to lead you, SHAME."

"What makes the court the authority on what is a civil right or not? Nothing."

"This issue was for the people and their representatives to decide, not seven rats in black robes. This ruling was unconstitutional and those so-called judges should be thrown out on their asses."

Chapter 6: Targeted Mass Communication

"Together we are going to win, and when we win everyone wins."
Jonathan Wilson, Des Moines Attorney
Friday Morning Breakfast Club — March 7, 2008

Some people hesitate to sign or send a form letter to a legislator thinking it will have little impact and most likely be ignored. Receiving a pile of form letters or a letter signed by a long list of constituents is fairly hard to ignore. I respond to constituents' form letters and, along with other legislators, have been known to cite the numbers received in support of legislation I am promoting.

There is no single profile for who sends form letters — the young and old, men and women, laborers and professionals, conservatives and liberals. Each letter comes printed from the same press on the same type of paper. Some letters have been copied and printed by the sender — content doesn't usually change. Form letters flood e-mail boxes. To save postage, form letters are often individually addressed and hand-delivered to the State House to be placed in legislators' mailboxes free of charge.

There was no shortage of form letters on both sides of the marriage equality issue. All have very clear messages in what they wanted me to do — even *demand* me to do.

One Iowa is the largest Lesbian-Gay-Bisexual-Transgender (LGBT) activist group in the state. Its postcard carried its familiar blue circle logo ink on its return address proclaiming "Together we are One Iowa". Someone delivered 200 of these postcards to me:

Dear Legislator,

Strong families are the backbone of Iowa's strong communities!

Today in Iowa, thousands of committed gay and lesbian couples are doing the hard work of building strong families every day yet lack the basic legal protections they need to take care of each other and their families. Committed couples lack access to health insurance benefits for their families and are denied the responsibility of making the medical decisions for a partner. These Iowa families need and deserve the protections and responsibilities of marriage to provide security, dignity, and a legal safety net for their families.

Iowa has a long tradition of and commitment to equality, fairness, and ensuring that all families are protected.

As an Iowan committed to fairness, I support marriage equality!

Signed _____

McCoy: Some form letters assume you are aware of the issue they are addressing. One such letter was brief and individually typed for e-mail.

"I'd like to request that you immediately encourage Senator Gronstal to let voters decide on an amendment to the Iowa Constitution. The Supreme Court's decision represents a sad day for Iowans and it would be nice if our elected officials let the people decide. The only reason not to is fear that your own agenda will not be upheld. As elected officials, do you lead by fear or by the will of the people?"

McCoy: There were carefully prepared petitions written in the format of a resolution.

IOWA MARRIAGE AMENDMENT PETITION

TO: State Representatives and Senators at the Iowa Capitol

Whereas: Marriage as established by God should be recognized by the civil power as legally, morally and historically between one man and one woman only; and

Whereas: A rogue Iowa Supreme Court has exceeded it proper constitutional authority, to claim legitimacy for so-called "marriages" of men with men and women with women, by usurping powers properly belonging to the legislative and executive branches of our state government; and

Whereas: Senator Majority Leader Mike Gronstal, House Speaker Pat Murphy, and House Majority Leader Kevin McCarthy have even gone so far as to use legislative rules and procedural power to thwart efforts to get a public roll call floor vote on the Iowa Marriage Amendment in either Chamber; and.

Whereas: Governor Chet Culver has caved in to and become an enabler of judicial branch revolution to try to overthrow the settled law, and the will of the people, on marriage in Iowa;

Therefore: I urge you to stand for marriage in Iowa as being between one man and one woman only, by casting your every vote, both procedural and substantive, in order to pass the Iowa Marriage Amendment through the Iowa legislature so that it can be put to a vote of the people of Iowa."

McCoy: A "protect marriage" e-mail received from many citizens urged me to vote "yes" on the Iowa Marriage Amendment House Journal Resolution 6 (HJR6):

"The truth is that social science demonstrates time and again, that children who are raised by their married biological parents do better, live happier lives, and contribute more to society than the children of any other family configuration. As a result, I encourage you to consider the needs of children and do everything possible to bring House Journal 6 to the floor vote. Oppose any weakening amendments, especially so-called 'civil unions.' "

McCoy: The statement about children is a complete fabrication. When a statement is made enough times, the hope is people will believe it.

McCoy: Citing supposed research to validate proposed positions is an often used ploy in political rhetoric as well as in form letters. Generalizations quoted from studies are often undocumented.

"...To re-define marriage and the family is to impose a dangerous undermining and lethal experiment on the entire society. This type of ruling opens a 'Pandora's box' to any other type of union that can enter the imagination of mankind and call it marriage and try to legitimize it.

- Studies have proven for the health of children they thrive best with a mother and a father.
- All other known civilizations have always had marriage between a man and a woman at their basic foundation, to do otherwise is cultural suicide.

- This is not a civil rights matter, sexual orientation is a choice and this type of court ruling establishes special privileges not rights."

McCoy: The following mass produced letters contained personal messages. Some messages were brief while others detailed the writer's story.

"When I was 19 it was a sin to be sexual outside of marriage. Even though I was not ready, I married my first relationship under that pressure. It was an abusive relationship. I was raped and belittled and my two daughters were sexually assaulted. Even under these horrible conditions my 'friends,' family, community and church pressured me to stay with my husband. He died of stomach cancer in 2000. The last two years I have been in a beautiful, loving, committed, nurturing, co-parenting relationship with a woman. Life is wonderful. Our kids are happy and thriving. I do not understand how that first abusive relationship could be a marriage and this current beautiful relationship is not."

"We are Americans and we are all created equally."

"I know gay couples that have been together longer than many married couples."

"We have been together for over five years, yet we still legally are considered single. We had to fill out a lot of paperwork just to get some of the rights straight people get just by signing their names on a marriage license."

"We have been together for 17 years. We applied for a marriage license on Day One when it was legal in Polk County. The court suspended the right to get married less than an hour after we applied. Civil unions are not enough. We want full marriage rights. We don't understand how allowing us to get married is going to hurt anyone."

"My parents have been in a loving, committed relationship for almost 40 years. When I meet that special man, I want to be able to enter into the same kind of union recognized by our government."

"Our six children and six grandchildren need to know that their family is not second rate."

———— • ————

"We have been committed to each other since 1984. My former wife supports us as do our children. We all celebrate holidays together. There are many kinds of families. We deserve the right to be legally married."

———— • ————

"When I was partnered, my wife and I knew if either of us was hospitalized we would not be able to make medical decisions for the other. I would not have even been allowed to visit her."

———— • ————

"Marriage is a civil right, not a religious privilege."

———— • ————

"Our eight year old son wants us to be married. He just does not understand why we can't and says, 'It's just not fair.'"

———— • ————

"Just as it was wrong to prohibit interracial couples from marrying in the 60s — it is wrong to prohibit gays and lesbians from marrying in the 21st Century."

———— • ————

"My sister is a lesbian. Her partner is as much a member of our family as the woman who is married to my straight brother. Both deserve the rights and privileges of legal marriage."

———— • ————

"It is a question of justice, equality, and fairness. It is important that people from different faiths speak up so that the

Christian Right's spewing of fear and hatred is not the only message heard."

———————

"It is the right thing to do. Isn't that enough?"

———————

"All people deserve the civil rights guaranteed by our Constitution."

McCoy: "Equality before the law does not translate into acceptance. Laws have to be enforced and when bigotry is involved, justice is rarely done." (ACCESSline, Jonathan Page, December 2013, p.26.)

———————

McCoy: The mass produced letters continue.

"We have been partners for 11 years. Our families bless us by accepting us as a committed couple. Each of us wears a number of labels: daughter, mommy, co-worker, partner, customer, citizen, voter, sister, and friend. We spend each day trying to fulfill the responsibilities of those labels. The one label we don't think about very often is the very label that prevents us from marriage and protecting our family and our children. The label that never comes up yet holds us down the hardest — gay. The gay label makes it twice as expensive and difficult to establish the protections that so many married Iowans take for granted. A straight couple doesn't even have to get married, if they just remain together long enough, their relationship will be awarded common-law status — bringing with it all the legal protections and benefits of a couple who participated in a wedding."

———————

"Next month I will be starting the process of changing my last name so that my partner and I share the same name. It will cost at least $100 to do so. We are saddened that we cannot just go to the Department of Motor Vehicles with a marriage certificate and change our name. We have to stand before the judge, after filling out forms and waiting 30 days, and explain to him or her why we want to do this. I have to share this very private and personal decision with a complete stranger and wait to see if I'm given approval. We would like to have children whom we will teach tolerance, pride and about accepting others no matter what their situation."

————

"As a heterosexual married couple, we both believe we are all children of God and deserve the same rights of marriage and love!"

————

"Imagine how you might feel if you were denied access to your loved one in the hospital or you could not make health care decisions on behalf of your loved one because you're not considered 'family.' Imagine if you lost your loved one and were denied access to their Social Security benefits or were denied inheritance of the home and life you built because you were not married. These rights are not extended to same-sex couples. It is time we assure these same civil rights to all Iowans."

————

"On Thursday afternoon, Polk County District Court Judge Robert Hanson ruled to overturn Iowa's amendment that denies same-sex marriage in the state of Iowa. In his 63 page ruling, Judge Hanson ordered the Polk County Recorder to start accepting and processing marriage licenses to same-sex couples effective immediately.

My partner and I had gotten up early and headed straight (no pun intended) for the Polk County Recorder's Office to apply for our marriage license before a possible stay was issued that would stop the recorder's office from accepting applications.

Friday morning we arrived at the Recorder's Office shortly after 7:30 a.m. we were cheerfully greeted by an enthusiastic staff that was already assisting a small crowd of gay and lesbian couples that had already arrived to do the same thing. We filled out our application form, and a notary public processed our application while we waited. The recorder was more than cordial and congratulatory as she handed us our copy of our marriage application certificate. I feel proud that I spoke up and thanked the couples that filed the lawsuit back in 2005 that Judge Hanson ruled in favor of just yesterday. Shortly past noon today, I was informed tha Judge Hanson had verbally issued a stay of his ruling due to pressure from the Polk County Attorney's Office. While I am disappointed that he did this, I am not disappointed that the legal process has begun."

McCoy: This form letter must have been miss-sent to me.

"CALL TO ACTION!! COME TO THE CAPITOL ON THURSDAY APRIL 9!

We just received confirmation from leaders in the Iowa House that tomorrow is the day that the first procedural vote to bring the Iowa Marriage Amendment (IMA) to the floor will occur. Now is the time for action! Gather with Christians, conservatives, and liberty-minded Iowans from across the state to personally urge every member of the Iowa House to vote for the IMA. Be sure to wear red to identify yourself as a supporter of marriage. Continue to keep pressure on the Iowa House by calling the following members who are still undecided as to how they will vote." *(Undecided members listed.)*

Chapter 7: Watch Your Back — we know where you live

"A man does what he must — in spite of personal consequences, in spite of obstacles and dangers and pressures – and that is the basis of all morality."
(*Profiles in Courage*, John F. Kennedy, Harper & Brothers, New York, 1961, p. 246)

McCoy: A threatening phone message was left in my office of employment in the heart of downtown Des Moines. Because the caller left a message for me there instead of at the Capitol, the investigation came under the jurisdiction of the Des Moines Police Department. The Reporting Officer was Sergeant Miller. His official report read:

Case Number: 09-11327

MCCOY RECEIVED A THREATENING VOICEMAIL MESSAGE ON 11 APRIL 09 AT APPROX. 1630HRS. THIS CALL CAME INTO HIS EMPLOYER — THE GREATER DES MOINES PARTNERSHHIP OFFICE LOCATED ON LOCUST STREET. THE CALLER PHONED MCCOY'S DIRECT EXTENSION LISTED ABOVE AND WHEN HE DID NOT RECEIVE AN ANSWER TO HIS CALL HE SELECTED THE #0 OPTION TO BE TRANSFERRED TO THE NEXT AVAILABLE PERSON. THE OFFICE WAS CLOSED ON 11 APRIL 09 SO THE CALLER LEFT HIS VOICEMAIL MESSAGE FOR MCCOY ON THE ASSISTANT KELLY'S PHONE. THIS MESSAGE WAS THEN FORWARDED TO MCCOY BY HIS SUPERVISOR MARY LAWYER. THE CALLER STATED "WATCH YOUR BACK WHEN YOU'RE OUT IN PUBLIC". THE CALLER EXPRESSED SOME DISAGREEANCE IN MCCOY'S SUPPORT OF A RECENT BILL PASSED IN LEGISLATION. THE CALLER MAKES SEVERAL DEROGATORY REFERENCES: "FAGS" AND "GAYS" THERE WAS NO SPECIFIC THREAT MADE NOR

ANY INDICATOR TO A PARTICULAR MEANS TO
FULFILL HIS THREAT. MCCOY WILL CONTACT THE
DEPARTMENT WITH CONTACT INFORMATION FOR THE
RUAN BUILDING TO OBTAIN ACCESS TO HIS PHONE
RECORDS IN THE LOCUST STREET BUSINESS. MCCOY
HAS BEEN ADVISED TO RETAIN THIS VOICEMAIL
MESSAGE UNTIL FURTHER INSTRUCTION FROM THIS
DEPARTMENT. IT WAS NOTED BY STAFF MCCOY'S
PLACE OF EMPLOYMENT IS ACCESSIBLE THROUGH
HIS CONTACT INFORMATION AT THE CAPITOL.

"Tool or Weapon Used: TELEPHONE."

"Method used: CALL."

"Crime: THREATS."

McCoy: An online article in the *Des Moines Register* (April 14, 2009):

"Des Moines police still don't know who placed a threatening phone call to an openly gay state senator Saturday. Someone threatened Sen. Matt McCoy in a telephone call to his workplace at the Greater Des Moines Partnership, according to a police report.

'The person is unknown,' Sgt. Vince Valdez, a police spokesman, said this afternoon. "There is no suspect.'

The voice mail message said, 'Watch your back when you're out in public,' a report says.

The caller expressed disapproval to McCoy's support of a recent bill. The caller made several derogatory references to 'fags' and 'gays,' the report says.

There was no specific indicator as to a particular means to fulfilling the threat, police said."

McCoy: *The Chicago Tribune* **(April 14, 2009) quoted the Associated Press:**

"McCoy confirmed it was a death threat, but declined to talk about details. Courtney Greene of the Iowa Department of Public Safety says McCoy met with state troopers at the Capitol, but because the threat wasn't received at the Capitol, it was referred to Des Moines Police. Greene says the patrol has received information that a number of lawmakers have been receiving 'troubling' calls and e-mails."

McCoy: Public reaction to this was questioning what has happened to our system when this kind of disagreement results in a threat? Where has civility gone? There was lots of angst. Empathy for my situation was expressed for having been out there and having to have endured this from a personal standpoint. It's the kind of thing that wears on you internally. Most people do not understand. People that spoke to me about it certainly shared with me they felt badly that it happened. I appreciated people saying it was a crappy thing to have to go through. People are genuinely concerned about legislators' safety due to the role we have taken to resist any amendment to the Iowa State Constitution. We couldn't be bullied into it. Name calling was part of that effort. Death threats were just another extension of that intelligence. I'm proud to say that nobody waivered. Everybody held together and stood strong on not voting for a constitutional amendment.

Essentially, what I know is that I received a great deal of conversation, protests and angst at the Capitol related to this issue. I met with worried constituents and individuals from all walks of life. I listened to their views and opinions in the Capitol's rotunda, on phone calls, in private meetings, and during one-on-one chats in grocery aisles.

One thing I've always found was that you could tell pretty quickly how a conversation will go with the person based upon how they framed their issues and the degree of passion with which they speak. I look for the anger in their message. Generally the veiled threats I received weren't so veiled. Some were very direct — "We are not going to re-elect you." "We are going to work to defeat you." "We are going to put up a candidate against you that supports our position." This is to where the angry comments would eventually evolve. There were individuals who would get into name calling. "You're queer." "You want to bring your queer agenda forward." "We're going to take you out." All this never bothered me too much. It made me uncomfortable for a moment, but generally someone is angry and unhappy when they are making threats. However, when I received the call from my boss that she had received a phone message that had been forwarded to her, I *was* concerned. This message and the way it was sent had crossed the line. It had been left on my phone in my office of employment. The message rolled over to my boss because at the time the Senate was in session and I was not in the office of my employment. I was at the State House. This ensured business messages were not ignored. The message essentially stated, in public you had better watch your back. We are sending you a message. You are wrong on this issue. You are running your mouth on this issue. You're not going to be safe anywhere. I turned the message over to law enforcement but wanted to keep it private.

Serving in the Capitol you learn quickly nothing is private. Information and gossip are the fuel for conversation. Before long the media had a hold of it and the word went out that I had received a death threat. I refused to confirm it with anyone but it still went viral.

The bottom line was that it was unsettling to think someone out there was apparently committed to doing me great harm. And yes, I literally watched my back. Routine travel routes were changed to avoid establishing recognizable patterns.

I understand this is the age we live in where individuals can make these kinds of threats and have the capacity to carry them out. You need only to look at Gabby Gifford and what happened to her at a town hall meeting. And know you are at equal opportunity for that same kind of deranged person to carry out threats in Des Moines. It takes only one mentally deranged person to come forward and do something like that. It has a chilling effect. It made me look both ways in a crowd and change how I wanted to open myself up to others. It changed how I attended public events and announced my town hall meetings. Why? This is because I don't want to be in a position where I could become a potential target for some disturbed person who happens to think I'm a sodomite. Being called a "fucking fag" or a "cheap sodomite" is less threatening than "You need to watch yourself in public, private and other places because we're going to bring harm to you." That's a whole different threat.

Law enforcement interviewed me. They took my statement. They also took and kept the phone recording. Their investigation tried to determine where the call originated. Was there an ID on the caller's phone? Did it come from a blocked number or from an identified number?

I don't know if they had suspects. Eric Baker, assistant to Senate Majority Leader Mike Gronstal, thought they knew who the caller was because others in the Capitol received threats. Calls were made to leaders considered out front on marriage equality. Senator Gronstal and Senate President Jack Kibbie each received calls at the same time I did. We were all outspoken on the issue and we were all correctly perceived as being opposed to a constitutional amendment to prohibit gay marriage.

You have to take it seriously or you should. Most did. This was not a school yard bully. This was someone who intentionally found out where to reach me as well as my phone number. Their going out to the public with threats created immense concern.

Changes were made at the Capitol as a result of these threats. Security was tightened. One change we noticed whenever we were in session was that a state patrolman was assigned to each chamber of the legislature. Their presence was increased around the Capitol. As I moved around the Capitol in and out of meetings I now had a heightened sense of vulnerability. A lot of times I was alone in a corridor. The Capitol is a very vast and open building. The metal detectors are a novel idea but we all know there are many entrances to that building where metal detectors are not stationed. If a person can get into another entrance in the building without going through a metal detector they can do whatever they want.

Steps were taken to provide more visible protection at the Capitol including officers accompanying legislators to their cars at night. While that is not something I did, I know others have sought this assistance from the Capitol police. Many security measures were not shared with legislators or public.

They coached me to be vigilant. Senator Steve Sodders, who is a deputy sheriff in his other life, told me to look for people who make a movement in a crowd, who launch towards me and to be ready to get out of their way. That was the strongest advice that he gave me. Don't put yourself in a position to be harmed. I limited my town hall meetings at that time and did fewer public things that would put me in publicly disclosed locations. It limited my access to my constituents. In light of the threat I didn't think it was the appropriate time to be doing town hall meetings.

When the doorman at the Capitol sent a note to my Senate desk saying there was a constituent to see me I went out only when the person identified themselves. I wanted to know who was out there and if possible why they wanted to talk with me. Thus, I avoided getting into risky situations with someone intending to do harm. Staff accompanied me to more meetings so I was not alone. There was somebody else visibly present at all times.

McCoy: E-mails and news items poured in with expressions of concern, anguish, and support.

"I'm from the San Francisco Bay Area but would like to extend my support to you for your stand on justice and equality. I just read that you received a death threat and as horrible and despicable as that is, please stay strong in upholding the freedom to marry in your state. As Harvey Milk had said, 'I fully realize that a person who stands for what I stand for, an activist, a gay activist, becomes the target or the potential target for a person who is insecure, terrified, afraid, or very disturbed with themselves.' Thank you for standing up for what is right." (California)

"Hey, Matt just wanted to say 'Hi cuz'. Saw your picture on the web for gay marriage, nice picture. Hope all is well. I heard from Mom that you are getting threats, the price you have to pay to be a leader of the free world, so they say."

McCoy —I responded: "Great to hear from you. Iowa is making big progress as it relates to gay rights and gay marriage. April 27th the Iowa Supreme Court has directed county recorders to issue marriage certificates to same sex couples as requested. My family is good and I hope that yours is doing great as well."

McCoy: From the *Mason City Globe Gazette* Editorial, Mason City, IA, (Tuesday, April 21, 2009):

"Irrational fears about same-sex marriage: It's been a bit more than a week since the Iowa Supreme Court ruled same-sex marriage to be legal.

The unanimous ruling stunned many and outraged others.

Protest yes, threat no.

Some same-sex marriage opponents have allowed their displeasure to take extreme forms. Last Monday, Sen. Matt McCoy, Democrat Des Moines, who is gay, confirmed that he had been the target of a death threat. Other lawmakers have reported receiving "troublesome" phone calls and e-mails.

Given the raw emotion involved, we can understand that a few people may say or write things without first fully thinking their ideas through. Threats of any kind, however, are the acts of cowards who deserve to be punished to the fullest extent of the law."

McCoy: This crisis brought contacts from previous years.

"I have been hearing your name quite a bit on the radio and thought I would look you up. I don't know if you remember me very well. I was on your floor — Alverno East — at Briar Cliff College from 1985–89. You were my resident advisor for a year or two. Anyway, I hope you are doing well. I am sorry to hear about some of the political problems in Des Moines — I guess that's politics. I have a wife and two lovely daughters and live in Lake City. Just wanted to say hello and see if you remember me. I remember a lot of late night conversations with you at Briar Cliff — you always stayed up late. Take care."

McCoy — I wrote back: "Good to hear from you. I remember you well. All is well in Des Moines and the Iowa

Senate. Congratulations on your family. I have a 10 year old son who keeps me busy. My Best! Stay well."

"For each wacko out there filled with hate, there are thousands of other people like myself who applaud your courage. I'm sending you lots of love from here in Massachusetts!" (Massachusetts)

"I read in the *Chicago Tribune* about your having been threatened. I am sorry people like the guy that called you even have to exist. Please don't stop what you're doing for gay rights."

"This evening I read a story on *Cedar Rapids Gazette Online* that you had been threatened. Thank you for being strong and willing to show the world that a gay man can be an honest, hardworking and trustworthy Iowa Senator."

"I am sorry you are the target of others' venom and hatred. Continue to stand for what's right. I'm in your corner."

"I read in the paper where you are being targeted. I'm proud of you for taking a stand and being who you are. Don't let a few filled with hatred get you down."

"Thank you for all that you do. Please do not let the words of those who fear change and fear a loss of power deter you from fighting for equality in Iowa."

"Just a quick note. I'm sorry you are having to deal with death threats and hostility coming from those who oppose us. I appreciate your work. I'm sure you'll have plenty of people watching out for your safety."

McCoy — I answered: "I appreciate your support and will continue to stand for human rights for all."

———————

"I just wanted you to know that, despite some of the crazy antagonists out there, you have the support of many people across this country and we are very proud of your work. Do not let those who toil away on the fringes of society deter you from standing up for what is right and just." (Las Vegas, NV)

———————

"Thank you, Mr. McCoy. And I apologize for the ignorant Iowans that have targeted you and your beliefs. I just heard on the news about the threats against your life. My belief is that God will judge those."

———————

"I just heard that you are getting death threats for supporting gay marriage/being openly gay. I am so sorry to hear that! I want to thank you for your openness. If more people were willing to stand up and voice their feelings openly this would not be such a huge deal. I include myself in this. A friend of mine is a big opponent of gay marriage here in western Iowa. I have been so upset with him that I can't stand it, but then I see him in person and I am all nice to him. It makes me hate myself later. Thank you for your strength."

———————

"Stay safe!"

———————

"Penis-sucking crap-eater. Die already."

"I'm terribly sorry and disturbed about your death threat — in the name of God, such a terrible thing.

McCoy: It is terrible, especially when we have a loving, non-violent God.

"*Advocate.com's* newsletter today told of the threat upon your life. I am saddened that Iowans would be guilty of anything like that. I am aware from first hand experiences, in the heated emotions over equality issues that one's perspective can fly right out the window." (Cleveland, Ohio)

"I was very disturbed to hear of the recent death threat. I am very proud of Iowa's recent ruling to support gay marriage. I only assume that the recent threat pertained to that issue. It makes me shake my head to think someone would have that much hate over this issue (or any issue, for that matter). I look forward to the day when prejudices are a thing of the past. Your positions are a healthy combination of critical thinking and common sense."

McCoy: The following letter was e-mailed to 46 Iowa State Senators.

"While reading a news article on your death threats, I realized how out of hand this has become. I ask each and every one of you to denounce this behavior of a person or organization that is resorting to scare tactics, including death threats, to put through their own agenda. I ask each and everyone of you to stand up and tell everyone this is wrong. Not only do I ask you, I challenge you to do this. Do the right thing as a human and as an

American to help stop these tactics and the hate that is being spread."

"After reading about the threat you received, I just wanted to thank you for everything you do on behalf of the GLBTQA community and women's issues. You are a strong and reliable advocate. I appreciate your progressive politics. Don't let the vocal minority drown out the voices of your supporters. We are with you."

"I read that you have received death threats from people who oppose extending equal protection under the law to same-sex families. There is nothing appropriate that I can say to you because I have never been in that situation. I am 26 year old and recently came out to my family. There have been ups and downs in this process, and sometimes when I'm feeling bad, I think about the LGBT people who came before me, who are older than me, and who had the courage to come out years ago. Things have changed so much since then due to the courage of people like you. The haters are using their dying breath to breathe fire, but just know that so many Iowans from all walks of life stand with you and are on your side."

McCoy: On April 14, 2009, *chicagotribune.com* carried an article, "Gay Iowa senator gets death threat" briefly stating I had received a threatening telephone call. "The threat was made as opponents of gay marriage continue to pressure lawmakers to take steps against a ruling by the Iowa Supreme Court that legalized same-sex marriage in Iowa."

The *Cedar Rapids Gazette*, Cedar Rapids, Iowa (April 14, 2009), stated, "McCoy was seen emerging from a meeting with law enforcement officials at the Capitol late Monday afternoon.

'That's all I can say, I've been threatened,' McCoy said when asked what the meeting was about, but confirming it was a death threat...The State Patrol has stepped up its presence at the Capitol, not only for the protection of legislators, but for other people visiting the Statehouse."

———————

McCoy: This e-mail is from a pastor with whom I exchanged several e-mails. My response to the pastor follows his e-mail.

"I am ashamed of that individual who made a threat to you and the audacity the person had to make a threat such as this. Let me assure you that this is not an 'approved' course of action and I do not believe it to be condonable by any group on any subject. I am sorry that politics has put such a target on you and I am even more sorry that depravity can motivate such a response from an individual.

I do understand that folks now are feeling like they are about to lose it all. You have had more than a logical amount of correspondence from me on the issue of gay marriage. I recognize you consider yourself a homosexual and as such I think you may have lost sight of the bigger picture. Marriage is not yours to toy with. While I don't agree, at all, with the threat you received or with anyone who would make such an action, I do feel that it should be considered as evidence that you must see that this issue is far bigger than you or your small group of cohorts. Historically, Americans have not been very happy with leadership who refuses to listen to them or give them their voice.

Again, I am sorry for the actions of a single idiot, or maybe even a group of them. I/we are not motivated by hatred, bigotry or malice. I am motivated by love. A love that looks for the effects this action of gay marriage will have on you, your lover, my family, society, the Church and me. If it is the will of the people to allow gay marriage then I will be silent. However, I want to hear their voice. Let us vote."

McCoy — I responded: "I am in receipt of your e-mail about gay marriage. While I find your comments interesting, they lack material argument related to due process and equal protection as the Iowa Supreme Court ruled that Iowa's existing DOMA violated. I do not believe that arguing about the Bible, morality or religious doctrine serves us well since there is a clear line which divides church and state. I would be happy to discuss any issues related to the Court's decision that relate to the material facts of the case.

With respect to your request to vote, you will have a chance to vote in the next election and it is your right to work to elect anti-equality candidates to the Legislature who will work hard to pass a Constitutional amendment to ban gay marriage.

You see, the will of the people is expressed through the election process and your current legislature does not wish to alter or amend the Constitution. I would encourage you, or others who feel similarly, to make your case to the public and run for the legislature.

McCoy: *To which the pastor responded*:

"With all due respect you cannot remove Church from State. If you remove my church you imply impose, in the vacuum, the Church of Matt, the Church of the Democrats, the Church of the Gay Agenda or whatever other opinion is being followed at the moment. When you use the term 'church' you simply mean a set of ideals. Which set is more dependable, those stemming from the church of Jesus Christ with its thousands of years of tradition, corroboration, and mimicking from other religions, or the Church of Matt or the Democrats which will change with the popularity and personal drive changes tomorrow. I cannot divorce my action from my beliefs. I ask you to look at the state's laws and tell me where they come from. I know you may say they came from a committee that met in our history but that committee even was governed by a set of values/morals. The values we have in this country derived from Biblical percepts and that cannot be denied. You may deny it if you like but the fact still remains that we measure right and wrong by the Bible. Any time we deviate from that Truth we will find ourselves in trouble. My friend, we must be bound to something greater than feeble personal whim."

"I apologize for the ignorant Iowans that have targeted you and your beliefs. I just heard about the threats against your life. My belief is that God will judge those. The ministers are not God and I see nothing wrong in same sex marriages…they are not life threatening."

"I have heard that you are being threatened due to the recent ruling in Iowa on same sex marriage. I live in Virginia. I am a woman married to a man, and we have four children. We live in a very conservative district, and a few years ago same-sex marriage was outlawed in our state. My husband and I support equal rights for ALL. We know the hate being launched toward you and others in Iowa right now will eventually be focused on us here in Virginia when we win OUR battle for equality." (Virginia)

"I am a bisexual American from Seattle currently living in Beijing. I recently read that you received a death threat, and I want you to know I am very sorry this has happened. Thank you for your courage and everything you have done and are doing for my rights and the rights of other LGBT Americans." (China)

"I am writing from Virginia to offer you the highest respect and gratitude for your strength in the face of the conservative backlash against Iowa's recent decision to extend basic rights to all Americans. While change can be difficult to accept, there is absolutely no excuse for childish and dangerous behavior, up to and including the recent death threats you have received. I am pleased to have learned much since the announcement about Iowa's long, forward-think legislative history. The rights of LGBT taxpayers are no longer fringe issues — they have been taken to the very soul of America where our LGBT friends, family, and neighbors have always been, waiting patiently for their turn to sit at the table. The time has come now for us to take our place as first-class citizens." (Virginia)

"Thank you for being an out politician and for your work in support of your nationwide family. Please know that Gay, Lesbian, Bisexual, Transgender and Questioning people across the country have your back in many different ways. Let your colleagues know we want and expect them to stand against bigotry and hate. Take what measures are necessary to secure your safety." (Virginia)

"I heard of the threats you received for your support of equal marriage rights. I support your fight against injustice. It is surprising how far people are willing to go in order to discriminate. These are cowardly attempts to deter you from your goal." (Sympathetic Virginian)

"Stay strong, you must. We need you in the fight for equal rights. You have countless constituents, organizations, and citizens in the US that look highly upon you, and are grateful to have a Senator with true courage, standing up for equality. It's amazing, because Harvey Milk was the first openly gay legislator elected, and had so much courage, and that's exactly what you remind me of. Gain police protection, and be stronger than the uneducated out there." (Arizona)

McCoy: Actually, Harvey Milk was the first openly gay man to be elected to public office in San Francisco and in the United States when he was elected as a San Francisco City

Supervisor. He was a trail blazer, a real pioneer, and a man of great courage, and sadly, a true martyr assassinated because of his sexual orientation.

Chapter 8: Post 4/09–The Fight for Justice Continues

"Justice has spoken. We have a lot to be thankful for."
Senator Matt McCoy

(Gateway Park Rally, Des Moines, April 3, 2009 following the announcement
of the Iowa Supreme Court's decision on marriage equality.)

"The only limits to our realization of tomorrow will be our doubts of today. Let us move forward with a strong and active faith!"

President Franklin D. Roosevelt
(Excerpt from undelivered speech prepared for Jefferson Day,
April 13, 1945. Roosevelt died April 12, 1945)

We've come a long way since April 3, 2009. A lot has happened. A lot more needs to happen. Iowans will continue to unite in following our state motto since 1847, "Our Liberties We Prize and Our Rights We Will Maintain." This motto has a new meaning to me. I am totally committed to our responsibility to maintain our newly achieved civil rights.

Stories in this book have humanized marriage equality. They are the stories shared by our friends and families. I've nodded in agreement with some, cursed some, and with others tears flowed. I felt their joy, pain, and yes hatred. I'm certain you did as well.

Although there is a shift in the country towards acceptance of marriage equality, there still lurks a danger the rights that granted equality will be repealed. We're talking about making fundamental changes in our society. The struggle for justice is not a done deal. We are at a turning point but major societal changes are not instantaneous. History reminds us that sweeping significant cultural changes may take decades to be universally accepted. Issues leading to the Civil War (1861-1865) are still being waged. That war ended 150 years ago but racial equality remains an on-going battle. The U.S. Supreme Court in Brown vs Board of Education (1954) ruled that separate schools for blacks and whites are not equal and therefore unconstitutional. Turmoil created over this ruling is still reported in the news.

Today's young people express disbelief that in our recent history African Americans could not marry whites. It's no big deal today. President Obama has a black father and a white mother. Years from now, I believe that thinking individuals will look back and say they cannot believe that we didn't allow same sex-couples to marry.

Injustice was in the air when the Chair of the Iowa Republican Party A.J. Spiker called for the removal of Iowa Supreme Court Justice David Wiggins in the November 2012 election. Wiggins was one of the justices voting in 2008 that Iowa's Constitution protected the legal rights of all regardless of their sexual orientation and thus supported marriage equality. The ruling was unanimous. In a mass purging, voters removed all three Iowa Supreme Court justices up for election in 2010 for having supported marriage equality. Two years later, Justice Wiggins survived the 2012 attack on him and was not removed from office. The intolerant words and actions hardly reflected the party of Lincoln that fought for the freedom of slaves and of Lincoln who issued the Emancipation Proclamation.

The entire marriage equality movement is fragile because it is new and things are moving so quickly. President Obama warned, "History can travel backwards." (Austin, TX April, 2014.) This is the civil rights movement of our day. President Obama came into office with the belief that marriage was between one man and one woman. While in office he made the decision to unilaterally ended the military policy that was implemented by President Bill Clinton of "Don't Ask Don't Tell." Through an Executive Order he ordered the Justice Department (February 23, 2011) to no longer prosecute under the Defense of Marriage Act (DOMA).

I credit the progress of marriage equality movement to social media — Facebook, twitter — with the awareness that has come out of its connectivity. An additional factor was the focus on youth. Same-sex marriage issues don't register as significant when tested on youth and those under age 35. Clearly, the president knew that his rise to power and this movement were propelled by that youth vote. Obama knew he had to deal with DOMA prior to 2012. I think he responded to that overwhelming majority of young people who said, "We don't get this opposition to same-sex marriage. End it." This decision by the president to take an affirmative position on marriage equality allowed him to seize this as an important issue to ride the tide for re-election.

Religious leaders continued to play a highly visible role in opposing marriage equality.

A full page advertisement was placed in the October 28, 2012 *Des Moines Sunday Register* by the Billy Graham Evangelistic Association. This was ten days before the presidential election. Billy Graham's picture occupied the lower half of the page depicting a very resolved man looking off into the future. Above his striking portrait, Reverend Graham signed the following statement:

"The legacy we leave behind for our children, grandchildren, and this great nation is crucial. As I approach my 94th birthday, I realize this election could be my last. I believe it is vitally important that we cast our ballots for candidates who base their decisions on biblical principles and support the nation of Israel. I urge you to vote for those who protect the sanctity of life and support the biblical definition of marriage between a man and a woman. Vote for biblical values this November 6, and pray with me that America will remain one nation under God."

McCoy: Father Erik Arnold, Catholic Archdiocese of Baltimore, pressed people to vote against Question 6 allowing gay and lesbian couples to obtain a civil marriage license. Speaking at a November 2, 2013 press conference Father Arnold stated:

"People of Maryland have come together to stand for truth that cannot be changed. Not always easy for us to proclaim our deeply held belief that marriage as created by God and given to us by nature should only be the union of one man and one woman. That our government does not have the right to redefine that truth. We have stood against the very powerful political forces and also the deep pockets of Hollywood and other special interests groups. But we know too the joy and power of being united in the truth about marriage. Unite across faiths, across races, across political parties and across time. I ask you to join me today in praying for our state and for our children and generation to come and join in prayer and we turn and let the Lord rein sovereign over this that his grace will be upon us, that his influence will be upon us, as we await the outcome of this very historic vote. We pray the Lord might strengthen our resolve. We pray that his will might be done on Election Day."

McCoy: God's will was done. Maryland voters approved Question 6 legalizing marriage equality.

Exit polling for the 2012 elections indicated 52% of respondents identified as Catholic voted for Obama and 48% opposed him. This after Catholic Church bishops invested an enormous amount of capital rejecting both ObamaCare for the alleged religious intrusion it made as related to contraceptives, birth control, and abortion procedures. It was also a rejection of the major theme of the Catholic Church that marriage was between one man and one woman. If you just looked at the Roman Catholic Church in the United States that once had pretty obedient parishioners, its members broke with their leadership and said, "Enough, we don't buy what you guys are selling and are not going to follow you on this."

This election represented an end of the Catholic Church's ability to dictate how somebody should feel or vote. Three Catholic governors also came out for same — sex marriage: Jerry Brown in California, Christine Gregoire in Washington, and Andrew Cuomo in New York. It was also a major defeat for religious conservatives' ability to impact elections. Those identified as religious Evangelicals were split 50 – 50 in the election as well.

The 2012 elections saw Tammy Baldwin of Wisconsin elected to the United States Senate, as the first openly gay elected official in the United States Senate. Victory Fund, whose mission is to finance campaigns for openly gay candidates running for office, has always felt that once the U.S. Senate was penetrated, the next office where we would see an openly gay elected official run, would be the Presidency.

One of the highlights of the 2012 election was the re-election of Iowa State Senator Mike Gronstal. Gronstal single-handedly, in a Senate comprised of 26 Democrats and 24 Republicans, withstood demands for voting for a constitutional amendment for more than two years. He endured constant bombardment and pressure to put same-sex marriage on the ballot. There were statewide petition drives, protests and demonstrations to get the state legislators to allow citizens to vote for a constitutional amendment on marriage equality. Gronstal withstood a barrage of church and religious leaders, including the Catholic Church, beating the drum saying this was something they wanted the right to vote on. Well over $310,000 in out-of state money was pumped into his opponent's campaign in hopes of defeating this champion of civil rights. Overwhelming support for Gronstal came from the people that knew him best, his constituents whom he had represented since 1982. It was one of his strongest victories and one for which he had vigorously campaigned. It was a huge victory for the State of Iowa. Senator Gronstal will go down in Iowa history as being a champion leader in this civil rights movement. He was later recognized with Interfaith Alliance of Iowa's Faith & Freedom Award.

A major positive change in the public's attitude toward marriage equality was evidenced in the 2012 elections. In all of the 32 states where marriage equality has been put to a vote it has lost. As of September, 2012, the six states that had approved marriage equality had done so through their legislatures or courts. In the 2012 presidential elections voters approved same sex-marriage in Maine, Maryland, Washington, and Minnesota. This was the first time it won voter approval. In seven states openly LGBT candidates won election to the state legislature for the first time. Huge.

On the day following the 2012 elections, Connie Ryan Terrell Executive Director Interfaith Alliance of Iowa declared:

"We stood together against the extremism of churches and pastors who crossed the line by politicizing the pulpit. We stood up to one pastor who threatened a parishioner and told his congregants how to vote in the retention election. Interfaith Alliance of Iowa stood in support of civility, religious freedom and separation of government and religion throughout this election cycle. Through the media, we used the strength of our combined voices demanding that those running for office and our elected officials not misuse religion as a divisive weapon."

McCoy: Stories need to be told and retold. They change the status quo as they humanize who gays are. When individuals get to know us, common ground is established and stereotypic prejudices begin to disappear. The following e-mail speaks to this.

"'You boys have just been real good neighbors; you're good kids.' That moment, that validation from a near stranger with whom my partner and I share a small slice of our life, made me realize we make the biggest impact when we simply live our lives openly, honestly, and naturally, just as our neighbors do in our modest, blue-collar Des Moines neighborhood. We've never tried to set an example, but somewhere along the way we did. In the midst of real life, came real understanding.

The most powerful tool we have in shattering stereotypes is simply being ourselves and inviting others into our lives. We have learned that there's a difference between pushing our views on others and simply living our life as any other couple would."

———————

McCoy: The divide over marriage equality continues and is not likely to pass quickly or quietly as illustrated by my e-mails in March 2013 with a resident in eastern Iowa.

"I am writing to urge your support for Senate Joint Resolution 8, a measure that would give Iowa voters the final right to decide the future of marriage in Iowa. In the four years since the court imposed same-sex marriage in Iowa, voters have made their displeasure strikingly clear. While voters in 31 states have passed marriage amendments affirming the historic and common sense understanding of marriage, Iowa voters have been denied that opportunity.

I urge you to make sure the marriage amendment is brought to a vote in the Senate this year. Support marriage as it's always been — the union of a husband and wife."

McCoy — *I responded*: I think gay marriage is wonderful in Iowa and will not support SJR 8. Get over it. Marriage equality is here to stay. Best wishes!

The writer quickly replied:

"If it's so great then why won't you let us vote about it? Gay marriage is simply a deception."

McCoy — *I had the last word in this earnest correspondence*: You don't vote on Civil Rights. That is why we call them

"rights." They are the same as your right to speak out
against something you don't like government doing. Even
when you're wrong it is your right to complain, protest and
argue. I don't have the right to silence your ignorance no
matter how badly I would like.

———————

McCoy: Conservative freshman Senator Dennis Guth is a
farmer from a northwestern Iowa community of 507. On
April 17, 2013, Sen. Guth spoke on the floor of the Iowa
Senate comparing the "gay lifestyle to second hand smoke."

Guth is on the board of the FAMILY LEADER/Iowa
Family Policy Center. He was active in "Let Us Vote," an
Iowa grassroots organization for a constitutional amendment
banning marriage equality. His concern for the "godless"
direction of our government has grown over the years. In
April 2009, when the Iowa Supreme Court issued an opinion
that same-sex couples could not be denied the "right" to
obtain a marriage license, he stated on his webpage, "I was
reminded of a quote from English philosopher Sir Edmund
Burke, 'All that is required for the triumph of evil is that
good men do nothing.' I knew I could no longer do nothing."

Guth's speech to the Senate:

"The media for the most part has bamboozled us to thinking
that having a relationship outside of the boundaries of
monogamous heterosexual marriage is positive, happy and
fulfilling. Back to the question, 'How do same sex relationships
hurt you?' This is similar to asking me, 'How does smoking hurt
you?' Just as there are multiple ways your smoking hurts me
such as secondhand smoke, increased insurance costs, costs to
society from days lost to poor health, so it is with same-sex
relationships. In talking to a young person, I would not want to
exclude the fact there are numerous health problems associated
with the homosexual life style. This includes sexually
transmitted infections many of which have negative life-long

consequences, ultimately shortening your life span. I would direct the youth to websites such as 'Facts About Youth' where they can find out more about the psychological consequences of this lifestyle...Bob Bergeron was a happy-go-lucky homosexual therapist who at the peak of his career committed suicide this past January. In a note found addressing homosexuality he said, 'It's a lie based on bad information.' Most of you know these things that I tell you are true but we have been intimidated into not speaking out. We all have a choice."

McCoy: Unbelievable. Once Guth finally shut his mouth I immediately rose on the floor of the Senate in response to him: "I was frankly taken aback by some of the things that I heard today as I know some of my colleagues were as well. I think it's important when we have these discussions about any topic, but particularly the topic of same-sex marriage, that we speak truth when we speak on the floor of the Senate. Much of what you heard today on the floor of the Senate is warmed over rhetoric that has been invented by the Christian Right extreme groups like the Family Leader and the Iowa Policy Center that have put together statistics related to health that just simply aren't true. In fact, the Center for Disease Control finds that the leading cause of sexual diseases is from the heterosexual community where promiscuity and multiple partners have led to rampant disease problems that are impacting society as a whole. I believe that all of us who are engaged in sexual activity have an obligation to teach young people about ways to prevent sexual spread of diseases. I think it is difficult to understand as a person that speaks with young people on a regular basis, how to impart to young people that choosing to be sexually active is a choice and when you choose to do that, being smart about it is absolutely essential. I'm talking about their health, but I'm also talking about their life and potentially the consequences that come from not protecting themselves. I think that we all have an obligation, all of us as adults, as parents, have an obligation to provide young people with accurate facts — something that the Christian Right and the

extremists have tried to keep out of our schools. Sexual education that would save lives and prevent disease has been banned from our public school system because of ignorance. While somebody cannot choose to be gay, you certainly can choose not to be ignorant and what I heard today was ignorant. And I know where it came from and I think that I am not gay by choice but I choose not to be ignorant.

———

McCoy: The reaction in the Senate to my retort was overwhelmingly positive. My remarks went national. The YouTube video of them has had more than 11,000 hits. Response to Guth's and my comments on the floor of the Senate swamped my Facebook:

———

"Guth should apologize to all Iowans for his false and offensive statements."

———

"I am disgusted and offended by Senator Dennis Guth's false and offensive statements about gay Iowans and Americans."

———

"All elected officials should aim to speak from a position that is informed, responsible, and accurate. Senator Guth's remarks reflected a profound ignorance of the facts, and demonstrated a lack of both tolerance and basic respect for human dignity."

———

"Claiming that homosexuality hurts him and his family in 'multiple ways,' as Senator Guth said, is just the sort of irresponsible, uninformed comments that fuels hatred, bigotry and even violence in our schools and workplaces."

"By comparing homosexuality to secondhand smoke, the only thing you convinced me of is that your speeches should come with a warning label."

McCoy — Bloggers quickly bounce into the fray:

"If I hear another person say 'homosexuality is a lifestyle' I'm going to flip some shit."

"Guth is a flat out ignoramus! I can't understand how he does not see the absurdity in his comments, let alone not knowing the facts about the research that proves the growth of STDs is in the hetero population. He is disgusting and should resign."

"Senator McCoy may not represent my district, but he certainly represents my attitudes regarding this issue. Although I cannot vote for you, you have both my respect and support. Thank you for responding to ignorance and bigotry with logic and dignity."

"Bravo Senator! Far too often no one will tell the truth so these lies about the dangers of this 'chosen lifestyle' — substance abuse, depression, shortened life spans and suicide — go unchallenged. What they don't seem to get, or choose to ignore, is that gay people might not be so depressed and inclined to self-medicate were we not treated so poorly."

"U r too nice — you shoulda told the asshole where to go and how to get there . . . it's no wonder I avoid the Red states."

"Thank you for being the voice of reason. Otherwise ignorant hate-speech would go unchallenged, and people would simply assume the person is telling the truth. You might want to ask him why he isn't demonizing straight teenagers who have unprotected sex. Our society ends up paying for millions of unplanned pregnancies every year. That's in addition to any venereal diseases they also get. I'd hate to have to label him a hypocrite."

"Thank you Senator. I am 22 years old and gay. You are changing our lives and paving for a better future."

"You're a better man than me Senator McCoy. I couldn't have been so gracious. When will these dinosaurs finally go away?"

McCoy: *The Victory Fund & Institute* **put out a placard, looking very much like a motivational poster, with my picture stating, "While someone cannot choose to be gay, you can certainly choose not to be ignorant. And what I heard today was ignorant. I am not gay by choice, but I choose not be ignorant." with quotation credits citing "Iowa State Senator, Matt McCoy."**

"*Progress Iowa* created a website with a poster picturing a standing, smiling Sen. Guth with a label stretched across his picture 'SENATOR DENNIS GUTH COMPARED HOMOSEXUALITY TO SECOND HAND SMOKE. TELL HIM HE'S THE ONE WHO SHOULD COME WITH A

WARNING LABEL.' The website provided people with the opportunity to sign an e-mail to Sen. Guth demanding that he apologize."

McCoy: All of this gives evidence that the battle for equal rights, for marriage equality is not a done deal. Vigilant preservation of our strides forward must be made or they can be destroyed. Strong inroads have been made as evidenced by the following developments.

On April 29, 2013, Jason Collins' coming out made bold headlines primarily because he was the first openly gay player in the four major U.S. professional sports leagues. Collins said he dealt with denial and anger in coming to terms with who he really was. But now he is the happiest he's ever been. Kobe Bryant, Los Angeles Lakers guard, tweeted to his many fans, "Don't suffocate who you are because of the ignorance of others." By being openly gay, Collins hopes to make it easier for others to do the same.

Jon Stewart quipped on his April 30, 2013 *The Daily Show*, "All in all it's a pretty great day for major league sports. At long last, they've decided that gay people are fit to be included in their elite club — one that's already allowed in adulterers, wife-swappers, gamblers, cheaters, rapists, racists, and slaughterers of man as well as those who've abused spouses, drugs, alcohol, family members and animals."

McCoy: As the highest ranking gay elected official in the state of Iowa, area media frequently contact me for comment on gay issues or events. The Des Moines Register columnist Bryce Miller wrote in an April 30, 2013 column, "Jason Collins walks same path as Iowa's openly gay senator." Miller made the comparisons that follow:

"Well, Matt McCoy did come out in 2003. In fact, the Iowa state senator remembers fighting knee-buckling nervousness as he approached the Capitol for a meeting with then Governor Tom Vilsack.

'It was awkward. It was a tough conversation to have,' McCoy said. 'He gave me great counsel and he gave me the courage to have that discussion with colleagues.'

A full decade later, the first man in a prominent American team sport summoned the courage to walk McCoy's sometimes rocky path.

'He's breaking the glass ceiling. He's changing the world by what he's doing, in his own way,' McCoy said. 'That's a major development. What Jason did, will allow other kids across the country to take that step.'

McCoy explained that the stigma of a person admitting he or she is gay exists — though lessens with each passing day. 'Every time someone comes out and shares their sexual orientation with the world around them, it opens doors for people that wouldn't have been opened otherwise.'"

As an Eagle Scout, I have struggled with the Boy Scouts' discriminating against youth on the basis of sexual orientation. Gay boys could join Scouts as long as they stayed in the closet in a "Don't ask, don't tell" approach. I am proud of my son who chose not to go into scouting because of their discriminatory practices. The decision was his — not his mother's or mine.

As of May 23, 2013, the Scouts' National Council finally, after a much divisive and highly public debate, allowed young openly gay men into its membership. However, Boy Scout leaders cannot be openly gay. This isn't good enough. They are still discriminating against adults who are being true to themselves in a world filled with diversity. These are

the very adults who can provide an important role model for tormented youth.

As is often the case when organizations or individuals take aggressive stands against gays duplicity is often uncovered. In October 2012, it was reported by the media that for decades the Boy Scouts of America (BSA) had covered-up sexual abuse by scouting personnel. Apparently they didn't get the memo prohibiting gay sex within scouting. The existence of their "Perversion Files," was made public. These secret and extensive files, with 14,500 pages, detailed cases of scout leaders banned from the BSA because of sexual misconduct. Hypocrisy is not limited to the Catholic Church.

———————

On June 26, 2013, the U. S. Supreme Court rejected the Defense of Marriage Act (DOMA) ruling same-sex spouses legally married may receive federal benefits. On that critical day, I spoke on the steps of the Iowa Capitol. Some of my comments follow. (My full address can be found in Appendix G, page 195.)

There is more work that must be done across the nation. As of today, 38 states have yet to embrace full equality for all. In more than 29 states a person can be fired for being gay, and in 33 states a person can be fired for their gender identity.

I have a message for those who have stood in the doorway blocking access to marriage equality. Your days are numbered. The future belongs to equality and equal rights for all. Today we celebrate our victory — tomorrow we get back to work!

———————

As of October 13, 2014, 28 states allow same-sex marriage: Alaska, California, Colorado, Connecticut, Delaware, Hawaii, Idaho, Illinois, Indiana, Iowa, Maine,

Maryland, Massachusetts, Minnesota, Nevada, New Hampshire, New Jersey, New Mexico, New York, Oklahoma, Oregon, Pennsylvania, Rhode Island, Utah, Vermont, Virginia, Washington and Wisconsin, plus the District of Columbia.

Arizona, Kansas, North Carolina, Montana, South Carolina, West Virginia and Wyoming could legalize same-sex marriage pending outcomes of federal appeals. Constitutional amendments or state laws ban same sex marriage in: Alabama, Arkansas, Florida, Georgia, Kentucky, Louisiana, Michigan, Mississippi, Missouri, Nebraska, North Dakota, Ohio, South Dakota, Tennessee, and Texas.

In August 2013, discrimination raised its ugly head in Iowa. A gay couple was refused use of a marriage facility in the Des Moines suburb of Grimes, a community of 9,040. Citing their personal religious beliefs, the owners of a public banquet hall refused two men the right to use that facility for their marriage. That's now illegal in Iowa.

That same month, New Jersey Governor Chris Christie signed a bill prohibiting licensed therapists from trying to turn gay teenagers straight. California is the only other state that also bans conversion therapy. A gay New Jersey Assemblyman labeled the therapy "a form of child abuse." In voicing a belief not in keeping with to his Catholic faith, Christie stated people are born gay and that homosexuality is not a sin. Christie demonstrates that change for social justice requires strong leadership willing to overcome resistance.

Also that month, the Treasury Department and the Internal Revenue Service said all legally married same-sex couples will be recognized as married couples for federal tax purposes and may file jointly. This will also apply to states where they live which do not recognize their marriage.

As recently as February, 2013, both houses of the Arizona State Legislature approved legislation that would have given business owners the right to refuse service to anyone if it would violate their religious beliefs. Gays were the obvious target. Supporters attempted to clothe the legislation in terms of religious freedom. But discrimination was written all over that bill. The Arizona Catholic Conference urged the Governor to sign the bill. Governor Jan Brewer vetoed the bill after recognizing that gays and their straight allies spend enormous amounts of money in Arizona.

Shocking but true, in North Caroline an employee can still be fired for being gay or for even giving off a gay vibe. This is almost amusing as only other gays are supposed to be able to possess "gaydar."

In early September, 2014, the State of South Dakota is waiting to award retirement benefits now available to same-sex couples following the U.S. Supreme Court throwing out DOMA. Their excuse is that court cases on the legality of same-sex marriage are pending in South Dakota. How those cases are determined will impact the South Dakota's Retirement System. Also in September, 2014, a federal judge in Louisiana upheld its ban on same-sex marriage. Clearly, a ruling from the U.S. Supreme Court is needed — and soon.

There are real threats. Gains can quickly disappear. Going into the fall 2014 state elections, Iowa Republicans hold the governorship as well as the House of Representatives. Democrats hold the Senate, but only by two votes. Those two votes can mean the difference in whether marriage equality and other critical issues will be supported or abandoned. Republican Governor Branstad, also up for re-election, has stated he does not support same-sex marriage and will support a vote by the people on this issue. A lot is riding on this election.

In a September 28, 2014 large bold headline the *Des Moines Register* admonished Iowa Governor Branstad proclaiming "RIGHTS SHOULD NOT BE UP TO A POPULAR VOTE". The sub-title read, "SOME OF U.S.'S DARKEST TIMES HAVE BEEN WHEN WE DENIED RIGHTS FOR SOME." (*Des Moines Register*, September 28, p. 10P.)

Monday, October 6, 2014 may not be a day remembered by future generations, but it will be a marker in the struggle for marriage equality. On that date the United States Supreme Court declined to hear three appeals from federal appeals courts that had declared same-sex marriage bans unconstitutional. The impact of this action is that it will expand same-sex marriage to 11 more states covered by these circuit court districts, bringing the total number of states for marriage equality to 30.

A Louisiana federal judge has upheld that state's ban on same-sex marriage. If that ruling goes to United States Supreme Court the Court may hear it as it will constitute a conflict of rulings among the circuit courts of appeals. It's unlikely the Court will rule in favor of bans on same gender marriage.

The New York Times editorial *Mistakes and Confusion on Marriage Equality* stated, "After Monday's nondecision — which had the effect of legalizing same-sex marriage in 11 states — there is little question where the court and nation are headed. Some opponents also see the writing on the wall, even in conservative Mississippi, where Andy Gipson, a state lawmaker, said, 'I am opposed to same-sex marriage, but I believe the time has come for people of faith in Mississippi to prepare for the overturning of our constitutional ban on it.'

The Supreme Court has dodged clear opportunities to decide the fate of same-sex marriage, and, in the process, harmed same-sex couples, their children and their families. Are the justices waiting for conflicting rulings from federal appeals courts to take up the constitutional questions? No one can be sure. But the court has the power and the responsibility to affirm the dignity and equality of millions of Americans, and it should do so as soon as possible." (*The New York Times*, October 10, 2014, p. EA-22)

In the meantime there is evidence that the number of Americans favoring marriage equality is growing with some pollsters claiming the majority now favor it.

That same week in which the United States Supreme Court declined to review those appeals, the Iowa Republican Party stated that it "stands firmly behind America's moral heritage of defining marriage as the union of one man and one woman."

Bob Vander Plaats, President and CEO of the FAMiLY LEADER, issued a statement to his followers on the same day of the U.S. Supreme Court's announcement.

Dear Friend of the FAMiLY,

…This morning's disappointing SCOTUS non-ruling amounts to a handful of appointed, virtually non-accountable Judges punting on their duty. SCOTUS had the opportunity to correct numerous, legally and morally twisted lower court decisions. Those judges' opinions fly in the face of 6000 years of human history, they disregard our Nation's founding legal principles of "…the Laws of Nature and of Nature's God," and they disrespect tens of millions of voters in many States, who passed Constitutional Amendments declaring what God, Nature, history and common sense all know: marriage can only truly be between one man and one woman.

The political ramifications of today's "punt" should be obvious. "We the People" are under attack regarding our rights of conscience, our religious liberty, and our very religious/moral beliefs which were shared by the Founders.

This overt, post-modern arrogance has led to much pent up frustration by the voters. It should motivate and necessitate our thorough vetting of candidates for public office, and of current officeholders, by pressuring them to tell us, "What are you going to do about this? What is your leadership strategy to right this ship? What's your remedy to this leftist takeover by judges, who are flying in the face of 'the Laws of Nature and Nature's God'?"

Furthermore, why would any governor or state legislature capitulate to these Judges? As Jefferson and Lincoln noted, judges aren't the most powerful branch of government. The other two branches have as much say constitutionally, and more say practically, than the judiciary. Where are the Lincolns and the Jeffersons of our era?

Strengthening families,

The FAMiLY LEADER team
Bob Vander Plaats,

In a letter to the *Des Moines Register*, Donna Red Wing, executive director of One Iowa, Iowa's largest gay organization, Red Wing stated:

"...According to a March 2014 Washington Post/ABC national poll, a majority of Americans support marriage equality. Also, because of Monday's decision, the door as opened for the freedom to marry in many more states under the same judicial circuits.

The tide is turning...May GOP leaders have already accepted that truth.

What's more, making claims of 'activist judges' is wrong, misleading and harmful to our valued judiciary both here in Iowa and nationally...As we celebrate this new reality for thousands of loving couples, we are reminded that

in our ongoing struggle for full equality, we are wining."
(*Des Moines Register*, October 10, 2014, p. 22A.)

"McCoy, You're Going Straight to Hell McCoy!" Well, I
don't think I'm going to hell. At least I hope not. During the
four years since Jim and I began this book changes in the
public's perceptions of same-gender marriage and of gays, as
individuals as well as a group, has been remarkable.
Although we still don't have a "Will & Grace" world, we
have more and more people willing to risk being open with
their sexual identification. One-by-one celebrities, neighbors,
and family members announce their sexual orientation
building on a foundation of tolerance enabling others to
accept themselves for whom they really are. Tolerance and
self-acceptance leads to an overwhelming feeling of freedom.

I hope readers of my story and of the e-mails found in
this book see themselves or others who are seeking
acceptance, truth, and the right to participate in the life
guaranteed to all citizens. Through this insight may they
become champions of the new civil rights movement. If we
have achieved that understanding, we will have been
successful. We know our unfolding movement will continue
forward because democracy works only when it works for
everyone.

Iowa has sent a strong message of equal justice for all.
We have defined the new normal for the future. We won't go
back. We can't return to living the role of second-class
citizens. To do nothing is to promote injustice. Let us build
coalitions for equal justice. Let us gain strength through
community and our collective self-confidence. Let us change
what is wrong. Let us put our words into action. Let us have
the courage to accept ourselves as we are. Let us continue to
retell our stories which engage the hearts of others to accept
us for whom we are. Let us not try to change ourselves to
meet the expectations of others. Let us gain strength from
knowing we're on the right side of history!

The continued fight for marriage equality is not a spectator sport. Do not turn over the struggle for equal civil rights — regardless of the cause — to others.

This is our moment.

Appendices

Appendix A: Iowa United Methodist Bishops Statement on the Iowa Supreme Court Decision, Bishop Julius C. Trimbe, Iowa Annual Conference of the United Methodist Church, Des Moines, page 180

Appendix B: Resolution 3-05A enacted in the 2004 Convention of The Lutheran Church — Missouri Synod (LCMS), condemned same-sex, page181

Appendix C: Iowa Catholic Conference Statement on an Iowa Constitutional Amendment regarding Marriage Updated April 2009, page 182

Appendix D: Interfaith Alliance of Iowa Action Fund Letter to Iowa Legislators in Support of Marriage Equality, February 16, 2010, page 184

Appendix E: MARRIAGE EQUALITY POLICY, Plymouth Congregational Church, United Church of Christ, Des Moines, Iowa, page 190

Appendix F: Senator McCoy's Speech following Iowa Supreme Court Announcement Legalizing Same-Sex Marriage, April 3, 2009, page 192

Appendix G: Senator McCoy's Comments on the day the U. S. Supreme Court rejected the Defense of Marriage Act (DOMA) ruling same-sex spouses legally married may receive federal benefits, June 26, 2013, page 195

Appendix A

Iowa United Methodist Bishop's Statement on the Iowa Supreme Court Decision
Bishop Julius C. Trimbe, Iowa Annual Conference
United Methodist Church, Des Moines

On Friday, April 3, 2009, Iowa became the third state to allow same-sex couples to marry...The stage is set for increased pressure on the state legislature, elevated debate about civil rights for gays and religious rancoring among those who chose a path of bitter discourse as opposed to prayerful patience that will continue over legality and morality.

I received a call asking me for a brief response for the media. I chose to give no response until I had time to fast, pray and reflect. It was my choice to speak first with United Methodists and I did so on Sunday and I did so at Wesley United Methodist Church in Muscatine, Iowa. At the conclusion of my Palm Sunday sermon, I shared a brief comment...

Our current *Book of Discipline*, paragraph 341.6, "Ceremonies that celebrate homosexual unions shall not be conducted by our ministers and shall not be conducted in our churches"...As we welcome a new spring as Easter people, we have questions to ask ourselves and new opportunities for dialogue and decisions. I have decided not to accept an invitation from Catholic Bishops of Iowa and other religious leaders in condemning the Iowa Supreme Court. I strongly believe the Iowa Supreme Court acted with judicial integrity in its determination that 'civil' marriage must be judged under constitutional standards of equal protections and not under religious doctrines or religious views of individuals."

Appendix B

Resolution 3-05A enacted in the 2004 Convention of The Lutheran Church Missouri Synod (LCMS), condemned same-sex (Edited for length)

WHEREAS, the LCMS, in convention, in 1973, stated in Res. 2-04 (Proceedings, p. 110): 'That the Synod recognize homophile behavior as intrinsically sinful" (Lev. 18:22; 20:13; Rom. 1:24-27); and

WHEREAS, The Synod, in convention (2001 Res. 2-08A), encouraged its congregations 'to minister to homosexuals . . .and

WHEREAS, Many in American society are demanding legal recognition of same-sex unions as 'marriages' by appeals to 'equality under the law' (e.g., the Supreme Court of the State of Massachusetts, Feb. 4, 2004); and

WHEREAS, Homosexual behavior is prohibited in the Old and New Testaments (Lev. 18:22, 24; 20:13; 1Cor. 6:9-20; 1 Tim. 1:10) as contrary to the Creator's design (Rom. 1:26-27); and

WHEREAS, For our Synod to be silent, especially in the present context, could be viewed as acceptance of the homosexual lifestyle; therefore be it

Resolved, That the Synod urge its members to give a public witness from Scripture against the social acceptance and legal recognition of homosexual 'marriage'; and be it further

Resolved, That the members of the Synod deal with sexual sins with the same love and concern as all other sins, calling for repentance and offering forgiveness in the Good News of Jesus Christ when there is repentance; and be it further

Resolved, That the LCMS, in convention, affirm, on the basis of Scripture, marriage as the lifelong union of one man and one woman (Gen. 2:2-24; Matt. 19:5-6).

Appendix C

Iowa Catholic Conference
Statement on an Iowa Constitutional Amendment regarding Marriage
Updated April 2009

"Marriage is a basic human and social institution. Though it is regulated by civil laws and church laws, it did not originate from either the church or state, but from God. Therefore, neither church nor state can alter the basic meaning and structure of marriage.

Marriage, whose nature and purposes are established by God, can only be the union of a man and a woman and must remain such in law. In a manner unlike any other relationship, marriage makes a unique and irreplaceable contribution to the common good of society, especially through the procreation and education of children...(taken from "Between Man and Woman: Questions and Answers About Marriage and Same-sex Unions," U.S. Conference of Catholic Bishops, 2003).

In August 2007, a Polk County District Court judge struck down Chapter 95.2 of the Iowa Code, which said that 'only a marriage between a man and a woman is valid' in the State of Iowa. At the heart of the judge's ruling was a finding that marriage is a fundamental right. Consequently, the state of Iowa had the burden of proving that it had a compelling interest in withholding marriage from members of the same sex.

On April 3, 2009, the Iowa Supreme Court upheld the decision of the Polk County District Court. According to its own summary, the Supreme Court directed 'that the remaining statutory language be interpreted and applied in a manner allowing gay and lesbian people full access to the institution of civil marriage.'

Because of this decision, we affirm that it is important to work towards the passage of an amendment to Iowa's Constitution which would define marriage as being between one man and one woman. Amending Iowa's Constitution requires that two successive General Assemblies pass the legislation, which would then put the amendment to a vote of the people of Iowa.

We are convinced that the passage of this amendment is important for the following reasons.

First, the institution of marriage as a union between one man and one woman goes back to the beginning of recorded human history. Marriage between a man and a woman is good from the perspectives of both natural law and our Catholic faith…

Secondly, we affirm that marriage is a gift from God which is essential to the stability of family and society…Children who are raised by a married father and mother have more positive outcomes, including behavioral and educational accomplishments.

Thirdly, unfortunately, in recent decades, cohabitation and divorce laws have already contributed to a weakening of marriage…

Fourthly, social engineering by judges or legislatures adds to the confusion about the good that marriage offers to society, and weakens the critical relationship between marriage and parenting.

Therefore, we call on Catholics and other citizens of Iowa to reflect carefully on the real social cost of this judicial imposition, and to support the need for a constitutional amendment. We affirm that this is the best way for Iowans to support the ideal of marriage as the stable union of one man and one woman."

Most Rev. Jerome Hanus, OSB, Archbishop of Dubuque
Most Rev. R. Walker Nickless, Bishop of Sioux City
Most Rev. Martin Amos, Bishop of Davenport
Most Rev. Richard Pates, Bishop of Des Moines.

Appendix D

The Interfaith Alliance of Iowa Action Fund
February 16, 2010

Dear Senators and Representatives,

As clergy representing a broad spectrum of theological beliefs, we join together to state our public support of civil marriage equality for same-gender couples and our opposition to any current or future legislation diminishing the marriage rights rightfully given by Iowa's Supreme Court. We are compelled by our deepest beliefs to stand for fairness in our common civic life. We oppose the use of sacred texts and religious traditions to deny equal protection and responsibility under the law for gay and lesbian couples.

From a religious perspective, marriage is about a couple entering into a holy covenant with their God and making a long-term commitment to share life's joys and sorrows. Moreover, as many faith traditions affirm, where there is love, the sacred is in our midst. This belief is the same for couples comprised of a man and a woman, two women, or two men. As such, a marriage based in love and commitment must be honored and supported.

Civilly, marriage is commonly valued in society because it creates stable, committed relationships; provides a means to protect and be responsible for each other; and nurtures the individual, the couple, and children. All families must be supported in building stable, empowering, and respectful relationships. Marriage equality is a means to strengthen families and is especially beneficial to children who are raised by gay and lesbian couples.

We affirm freedom of conscience in this matter. Marriage equality honors the religious convictions of those communities and clergy who officiate at, and bless, same-gender marriages. We recognize the state does not and should not require clergy or religious traditions who disagree with same-gender marriage to officiate at, or bless, the ceremonies of gay and lesbian couples. The state must respect the convictions of all religious groups and individuals, while also allowing the fundamental right of marriage to be granted fairly to all people.

As clergy, we stand together in support of civil marriage equality for ALL families. We ask for your support of civil marriage equality and ask that you oppose any resolution or attempt to diminish the marriage rights of Iowa's families.

(Inclusion of signatory's congregation, organization, or denomination is for identification purposes only.)

With appreciation,

Bishop Alan Scarfe; Bishop; Episcopal Diocese of Iowa
Rev. Dr. Rich Pleva; Iowa Conference Minister; United Church of Christ
Rev. Dr. Richard Guentert; Former Regional Minister of the Upper Midwest Region (retired); Christian Church (Disciples of Christ)
Rev. Charles Ager; ELCA (retired); Strawberry Point
The Rev. Alexander A. Aiton, Jr.; Rector, St. John's by the Campus Episcopal Church & Student Center; Ames
The Rev. Dr. James Altenbaumer; United Church of Christ; Cedar Falls
Rev. Nancy L. Anderson; Zion United Church of Christ; Hubbard
Rev. Michael N. Armstrong; Senior Minister; First Christian Church (Disciples of Christ); Davenport
Rev. Paul S. Bengtson; ELCA (retired); Storm Lake
Rev. Steve Bibb; First United Methodist Church; Fort Dodge
Rev. Anna Blaedel; United Methodist Church; Osage
Rev. Ramona S. Bouzard; St. Paul Lutheran Church; Waverly
Rev. Dr. Walter C. Bouzard; Waverly
Rev. Stephen L. Bowie; Member, Presbytery of Des Moines; Bloomfield
Pastor Brad Braley; First Presbyterian Church; Cedar Falls
Rev. Kenneth E. Briggs, Jr.; Chaplain, Lt. Col, USAF (retired); Altoona Christian Church (DOC); Altoona
The Rev. Jeanette Brodersen; Associate Minister, Plymouth Congregational United Church of Christ; Des Moines
Rev. Barbara Bullock; United Church of Christ (retired); Ankeny
The Rev. Dr. Sean D. Burke; Luther College; Decorah
Rev. Christopher C. Burtnett; Schleswig United Church of Christ; Schleswig
Rev. Linda M. Butler; Collegiate United Methodist & Wesley Foundation; Ames
The Rev. Dr. Robert A. Butterfield; Urbandale United Church of Christ; Urbandale
Rev. Eva S. Cameron; Unitarian Universalist Society of Black Hawk County; Cedar Falls
Reverend Tom Capo; Peoples Church Unitarian Universalist; Cedar Rapids
Pastor John Chaplin; Licensed Pastor; Central Association of the Iowa Conference of the United Church of Christ; Des Moines
Rev. Kathleen Clark; United Methodist Church (retired); Des Moines

*Priest Richard Cleaver; Saints Ephrem and Macrina Mission, Orthodox-
    Catholic Church of America; Grinnell*
Rev. Dr. David Cline; Evangelical Church in America; Polk City
Rev. Milton Cole Duvall; Episcopalian; West Des Moines
Rev. Elizabeth Colton; United Church of Christ; Oskaloosa
Dr. Rev. Robert Cook; Presbyterian Church, U.S.A. (retired); Des Moines
Rev. William Cotton; United Methodist Church (retired); Des Moines
*Rev. Robert S. Crandall; Executive Director; Bidwell Riverside Center; Des
Moines*
Pastor Michael Dack; United Church of Christ; Newton
Rev. D. Mark Davis; Pastor, Heartland Presbyterian Church; Clive
*Rev. Pamela S. Deeds; Walnut Hills United Methodist Church/ Wesley
UMC's; Des Moines*
Rev. Dennis Dickman; ELCA (retired); Waverly
*Rev. Dr. Tim Diebel; First Christian Church (Disciples of Christ); Des
Moines*
*Rev. Elizabeth Dilley; First Congregational United Church of Christ; Red
Oak*
Rev. Barbara Dinnen; United Methodist Church; Des Moines
*The Rev. Maureen Doherty; Cedar Valley Episcopal Campus Ministry; Cedar
Falls*
*Sondra Eddings; Minister; Christian Church (Disciples of Christ); Des
Moines*
Rabbi Steven Edelman-Blank; Tifereth Israel Synagogue; Des Moines
Rev. Dr. Brian Eslinger; Unitarian Universalist Fellowship of Ames; Ames
Rev. Peg Esperenza; Church of the Holy Spirit, MCC; Des Moines
*Rev. Faith Ferre'; Minister of Discipleship, Plymouth Congregational United
    Church of Christ; Des Moines*
Rev. Jeffrey E. Filkins; Trinity United Church of Christ; Hartley
The Rev. Travis M. Fisher; St. Mark Lutheran Church; Davenport
Rev. Dr. Barbara Gaddis; Collegiate Presbyterian Church; Ames
The Rev. Andrew G. Gangle; Peace Lutheran Church; Adel
Rev. Fred R. Gee; retired, Christian Church (Disciples of Christ); Des Moines
Reverend Tom Gehlsen; Episcopal Diocese of Iowa; Des Moines
Rev. Randall E. Gehring; Bethesda Lutheran Church, ELCA; Ames
*Rev. Jaymee Glenn-Burns; Field Outreach Minister, United Methodist
Church; Cedar Falls*
Rev. David Glenn-Burns; Wesley Foundation at UNI; Cedar Falls
Rabbi Guy Greene; Congregation Beth Shalom; Sioux City
The Rev. John H. Greve; New Song Episcopal Church; Coralville
Rev. Chet Guinn; Methodist Federation for Social Action; Des Moines
Rev. Elizabeth Gull; Universal Life Church; Nevada
Rev. Susan Guy; United Methodist; Urbandale
Pastor John Hagberg; St. Mark Lutheran Church; Sioux City
*The Rev. Jennifer L. Hall; Chaplain, Iowa Health; Metropolitan Community
Churches; Des Moines*

Rev. Dawn Halstead; Chaplain, Hospice of Central Iowa; Des Moines
Rev. Bob Hamilton; United Church of Christ (retired); Davenport
Rev. George Hanusa; ELCA (retired); Windsor Heights
Rev. Richard W. Harbart; United Church of Christ; Clive
The Rev. John Harper; New Song Episcopal Church; Coralville
Rev. Stephanie Haskins; Associate Minister, Plymouth Congregational United
    Church of Christ; Des Moines
Rev. Nicole Havelka; Iowa Conference United Church of Christ; Des Moines
Rev. Mark Haverland; United Methodist Church; Ankeny
Rev. Dave Heinze; Campus Minister; Graceland University; Lamoni
Rev. Rich Hendricks; Metropolitan Community Church of the Quad Cities;
Davenport
Rev. Dan Herndon; United Methodist Church (retired); Waterloo
Dr. Susan E. Hill; Associate Professor of Religion, UNI; Unitarian
    Universalist Society of Black Hawk County; Waterloo
The Rev. Holly Horn, PhD; Tiffin
Rev. Margaret Hutchens; First Christian Church (Disciples of Christ);
Charles City
Rev. Gerald Iverson; Associate in Ministry; ELCA (retired); Sioux City
Pastor Steven M. Jacobsen; First Lutheran Church; Decorah
Rev. Carlos Jayne; United Methodist Church (retired); Des Moines
Rev. Eric Johnson; Reformed Church in America; Des Moines
Reverend Patricia Johnson; Episcopal Deacon; Sioux City
Rev. Paul A. Johnson; United Church of Christ - Congregational; Ames
The Rev. Scott A. Johnson; Lutheran Campus Ministry at Iowa State
University (ELCA); Ames
Rev. R. Paul Johnston; Trinity Lutheran Church (ELCA); Sioux City
The Rev. Dr. Judith Jones; St. Andrew's Episcopal Church; Waverly
Rabbi Henry Jay Karp; Temple Emanuel; Davenport
Rabbi David Kaufman; Temple B'Nai Jeshurun; Des Moines
The Rev. Robert Keefer, PhD; Presbyterian; Clarinda
Rev. Naomi Kirstein; Wellspring Community Church; Des Moines
Rev. Bruce Kittle; Faith United Church of Christ; Iowa City
The Rev. Dr. Kathryn A. Kleinhans; Wartburg College; Waverly
Pastor Jim Klosterboer; Bethany Evangelical Lutheran Church; Elkader
Rev. C. Eugene Koth; United Methodist Church (retired); Clive
Rev. Mark W. Kukkonen; Intentional Interim Pastor; St. Stephen's Lutheran
Church; Cedar Rapids
Rev. Carmen Lampe-Zeitler; United Methodist Church; Des Moines
Rev. Martha E. Lang; Deacon; Trinity Episcopal Church; Muscatine
The Rev. Torey Lightcap; Rector, St. Thomas Episcopal Church; Sioux City
Rev. Kathleen Love, D.D.; Interfaith Minister; The Wedding Chapel; Des
Moines
Rev. James Love, D.D.; Interfaith Minister; The Wedding Chapel; Des Moines
The Rev. William H. Lovin; Congregational United Church of Christ; Iowa
City

Rev. Ted Lyddon Hatten; Wesley Foundation, Drake University; Indianola
Rev. Whit Malone; Collegiate Presbyterian Church; Ames
Rev. Mary Beth Mardis-LeCroy; Plymouth Congregational United Church of
Christ; Des Moines
Rev. Matthew J. Mardis-LeCroy; Plymouth Congregational United Church of
Christ; Des Moines
Pastor Sam Massey; First Presbyterian Church; Iowa City
Rev. Gene Matthews; United Methodist Church (retired missionary)
The Reverend Benjamin Maucere; Unitarian Universalist Society of Iowa
City; Iowa City
The Rev. Jean McCarthy; Rector; Episcopalian; Des Moines
Rev. Diane McClanahan; Trinity United Methodist Church; Des Moines
Rev. James I. Meadows, Jr.; First Congregational United Church of Christ;
Fort Dodge
The Rev. Russell Melby; Iowa Director, Church World Service/CROP; ELCA
clergy;
Rev. Fritz Mellberg; United Church of Christ; Hiawatha
John Miller; Commissioned Lay Minister; Unitarian Universalist Society of
Black Hawk County; Cedar Falls
Reverend Roger Mohr; Unitarian Universalist Fellowship; Burlington
Rev. Mary Moore; Unitarian Church of Davenport; Davenport
Rev. Allen Mothershed; United Church of Christ; Davenport
Rev. Katherine Mulhern; Edwards Congregational United Church of Christ;
Davenport
Rev. Amy E. E. Murray, BCC; Urbandale United Church of Christ;
Urbandale
Pastor Vernon H. Naffier; Faculty, GrandView University; ELCA; Ankeny
Rev. Peter T. Nash, PhD; Professor of Religion & Liberal Studies; Wartburg
College; Waverly
Rev. Gus Nelson; Presbyterian (retired); Des Moines
Rev. Barbara Nish; Presbyterian Church, U.S.A.; Des Moines
Rev. Patricia Adams Oberbillig; Minister of Pastoral Care (retired),
Plymouth Congregational United Church of Christ; Des Moines
Rev. Delwyn L. Olivier; Augustana Lutheran Church; Sioux City
Rev. Ronald Osborne; Des Moines
Rev. James R. Pemble; United Methodist Church (retired); Des Moines
The Rev. Doug Peters; Senior Minister, Walnut Hills United Methodist
Church; Urbandale
Rev. Oren Peterson; Unitarian Universalist (retired); Des Moines
Rev. Ronald D. Petrak; United Methodist Church (retired); Des Moines
Rev. Julie M. Poore; United Methodist Church; Granger
Rev. Charles M. Pope; Rector; St. Paul's Episcopal Church; Grinnell
Rabbi Jeff Portman; Agudas Achim Congregation; Iowa City
Rev. Robert Price; retired; Newton
The Rev. Catherine Quehl-Engel; Episcopalian; Mt. Vernon
The Rev. Julia Rendon; Crossroads United Church of Christ; Indianola

The Rev. Charity Rowley; Unitarian Universalist (retired); Iowa City
Rev. Nancy Ruby; Unitarian Universalist Fellowship of Clinton; Clinton
The Reverend Dr. David R. Ruhe; Plymouth Congregational United Church of Christ; Des Moines
Rev. Janette Scott; Presbyterian; Des Moines
Rev. Michael J. Schmidt; Christ Lutheran/St. Peter; LeMars
Pastor Victoria Shepherd; Denver
Rev. Charlotte Shivvers; Unitarian Universalist (retired); Knoxville
Rev. Deanna Shorb; College Chaplain; Grinnell
Rev. Diana Jacobs Sickles; ELCA (retired); Des Moines
Rev. Gary Sneller; First Christian Church (Disciples of Christ); Ottumwa
Rev. Dr. Larry W. Sonner, D.Min.; United Methodist Church (retired); Urbandale
Rev. Ron Spears; Retired clergy; Waterloo
Pastor Sarah Stadler-Ammon; Denver
Rev. Jerry Stevenson; Welsh Congregational Church UCC; Iowa City
Rev. William Steward; Grace United Methodist Church; Des Moines
Rev. Jane Stewart; New Song Episcopal Church; Coralville
Rev. Gayle V. Strickler, Jr.; Adjunct Minister for Community Concerns, Urbandale United Church
    of Christ; Urbandale
Rev. Mark Stringer; First Unitarian Church; Des Moines
Rev. Cheryl R. Thomas; Calvary Baptist Church; Des Moines
The Rev. Rachel Thorson Mithelman; St. John's Lutheran Church; Des Moines
Rev. Dr. James L. Wallace; Central Presbyterian Church; Des Moines
Pastor Barbara Weier; Zion United Church of Christ; Hartley
Rev. Dr. Susan K. Weier; United Church of Christ; Grinnell
Pastor Kenneth C. Wells; Licensed Lay Pastor; First Congregational UCC Church; Onawa
Pastor Mary A. Wells; Licensed Lay Pastor; First Congregational UCC Church; Onawa
Rev. Jane A. Willan; Zion United Church of Christ; Burlington
Rev. Dr. Dana Wimmer; Waterloo First United Methodist Church; Waterloo
Rev. Angie Witmer; Minister to Young Adults & Youth, Plymouth
    Congregational United Church of Christ; Des Moines
Rev. Beverly J. Wolff; St. John Lutheran Church; Cushing
The Rev. Jean Wollenberg; Executive Director/Chaplain, Hospice of
    Washington County; Washington
Rev. Bob Wollenberg; United Presbyterian Church; Washington
Rev. Mark A. Young; Wesley United Methodist Church; Ottumwa

Appendix E

MARRIAGE EQUALITY POLICY
Plymouth Congregational Church Council
United Church of Christ
Des Moines, Iowa

WHEREAS, the United Church of Christ has a long and proud history of leading the way for the expansion of human rights, including early opposition to slavery and the oppression of women, and

WHEREAS the United Church of Christ was the first American denomination to ordain an African American minister (1785) and the first female pastor (1853), and

WHEREAS in 1972 the United Church of Christ became the first denomination in America to ordain an openly gay man, and

WHEREAS in 1985 the General Synod of the United Church of Christ passed a resolution that called on congregations to declare themselves open to and affirming of gay, lesbian and bisexual people in the full life and ministry of the church, and

WHEREAS Plymouth Congregational Church in Des Moines became an Open and Affirming congregation in 1993, and has been recognizing commitment ceremonies of same sex couples since that time, and

WHEREAS, in 2005 the General Synod of the United Church of Christ adopted the resolution "Equal Marriage Rights for All" calling upon all settings of the United Church of Christ to engage in "serious, respectful, and prayerful discussion of the covenantal relationship of marriage and equal marriage rights for couples regardless of gender," and

WHEREAS the life and example of Jesus of Nazareth provides a model of radically inclusive love and abundant welcome for all; and

WHEREAS we proclaim ourselves to be listening to the voice of a Still Speaking God who calls us to work for justice for those who are marginalized; and

WHEREAS civil marriage carries with it significant access to institutional support, rights and benefits; and

WHEREAS equal marriage rights for couples regardless of gender is an issue deserving of serious, faithful discussion by people of faith, taking into consideration the long, complex history of marriage and family life, layered as it is with cultural practices, economic realities, political dynamics, religious history and biblical interpretation;

THEREFORE LET IT BE RESOLVED, that Plymouth Congregational Church of the United Church of Christ affirms equal access to the basic rights, institutional protections and quality of life conferred by the recognition of marriage; and

LET IT BE FURTHER RESOLVED, that the officers, ministers and members of Plymouth Congregational Church of the United Church of Christ are called upon to communicate this resolution to appropriate local, state and national legislators, urging them to support equal marriage rights for couples regardless of gender.

January 26, 2010

Appendix F

Senator McCoy's Speech following Iowa Supreme Court Announcement
Legalizing Same-Sex Marriage
April 3, 2009

Hello. I'm Matt McCoy. I represent the south side of Des Moines, Senate District 31 in the Iowa Senate. I'm a lifelong Iowan, an Eagle Scout, a community development director, a father, and the first openly gay member of the Iowa Legislature.

Today is a red letter day for the State of Iowa. All of Iowa's citizens now have equal protection under the law. Thousands of Iowans who have worked hard, raised families, and paid taxes will now be afforded the opportunity to marry. Fair minded people throughout our state support equality for all.

I have never been more proud of all the Iowans who have worked continuously for the advancement of human rights for all.

Today, we in Iowa are sending a message to all Americans, gay and straight. If you are looking for a great place to live, a place where people treat their neighbors with respect, please consider coming to Iowa to work, to invest and to raise a family.

Unlike the fight in California, I believe that this issue is settled in Iowa. Iowans will move on to fixing our economy, providing health care to our citizens and making our state a better place to live.

Here's why I believe Iowa will not go backwards when it comes to civil rights.

First — Iowa has a long history of civil rights leadership:

- In 1839, the Iowa Supreme Court rejected slavery in a decision that found that a slave named Ralph became free when he stepped on Iowa soil, 26 years before the end of the Civil War decided the issue.

- In 1868, the Iowa Supreme Court ruled that racially segregated "separate but equal" schools had no place in Iowa, 85 years before the U.S. Supreme Court reached the same decision.

- In 1869, Iowa became the first state in the union to admit women to the practice of law.

- In 1873, the Iowa Supreme Court ruled against racial discrimination in public accommodations, 91 years before the U.S. Supreme Court reached the same decision.

Second — social conservatives have made their case to Iowans and been rejected.

- The Iowa Republican Party is one of the most conservative in the country. For example, the Republican winners of the Iowa Presidential Caucuses include Pat Robertson, Pat Buchanan, and Mike Huckabee.

- Here in Iowa, the Republican Party has focused on fringe issues for some time. Iowans have responded by electing Democrats.

- In less than a decade, legislative debate has moved from considering laws banning gay Iowans from adopting children or being foster parents to passage of legislation protecting children from bullying in schools, expanding Iowa's civil rights protections to include sexual orientation and transgender, a vote AGAINST amending the Constitution to ban gay marriage, and, now, a court decision providing full marriage equality.

Third — the Iowa Constitution can't be changed quickly.

- As I said, we've already had one vote in the Iowa Senate on amending the constitution to ban gay marriage and that failed. That was when Republicans had the majority. Every Democrat voted no and enough Republicans joined us to defeat the idea.

- Now Democrats control the Iowa House and Senate, and legislative leaders say the issue won't come up for vote.

- Even if it does, Constitutional Amendments must be approved by two different two-year General Assemblies before they go to the people for a vote.

- In short, there is no way a flood of out-of-state money can be used to quickly scare Iowans into going backwards on civil rights.

I believe marriage equality is here to stay. Iowans will quickly realize that it is no big deal.

I'm so proud to be an Iowan today. Thanks for celebrating with us. And whether you're gay or straight, think about coming to Iowa to get married.

Appendix G

Senator McCoy's Comments on the day the U. S. Supreme Court rejected the Defense of Marriage Act (DOMA) ruling that same-sex spouses legally married may receive federal benefits
June 26, 2013

"Today is a great day for equality for the nation and Iowa. We owe a debt of gratitude to Edith Windsor who on behalf of her deceased partner of 42 years, Thea Clara Spyer, had the courage and audacity to demand equal treatment in inheritance tax laws.

Today's Supreme Court decision on the Federal legislation — the Defense of Marriage Act (DOMA) is a monumental moment in American history. Civil rights leader Martin Luther King said, 'The arch of the moral universe is long but it bends toward justice.' The fight never ceases. Today's rejection of DOMA by the Supreme Court closes a door on government sanctioned and condoned discrimination, and today the Court ruled that marriage equality is the law of the land. Our Federal government cannot discriminate between gay and heterosexual married couples. Our love is equal. Our citizenship is equal. Today, more than 1,100 federal rights and benefits have been extended to gay families in pro-equality states across the nation, such as:

- Health insurance and pension protections for federal employees' spouses,
- Social security benefits for widows and widowers,
- Support and immigration protections for bi-national couples,
- Benefits for military spouses, and
- Joint income tax filing and exemption from federal estate taxes.

I know the Iowa Supreme Court's decision in Varnum was an important national legal precedent that served as a blueprint for the US Supreme Court. The Iowa Supreme Court had tremendous courage in their unanimous decision on Varnum. Three justices sitting on that court, Marsha Ternus, Michael Streit, and David Baker, paid a dear price for having the courage to do their jobs with conviction.

There is more work that must be done across the nation. As of today, 38 states have yet to embrace full equality for all. In more than 29 states a person can be fired for being gay, and in 33 states a person can be fired for their gender identity.

I have a message for those who have stood in the doorway blocking access to marriage equality. Your days are numbered. The future belongs to equality and equal rights for all. Today we celebrate our victory — tomorrow we get back to work!"

Acknowledgements

Elvin McDonald, author of numerous publications and articles, for suggestions on writing, authors, and publishing.

Dr. Loren Olsen, author of *Finally Out: Letting Go of Living Straight*, for early coaching.

Sean Stubb, author of *Body Counts: A Memoir of Politics, AIDS, and Survival*, for critiquing the manuscript.

Jonathan Wilson, Des Moines attorney, for legal advice.

Natalie Dorn, free lance editor, for early editing.

Jill Ferguson for endless editing, patiently responding to hundreds of questions, and for unending support.

Bibliography

Barr, Cameron, Associate Minister, *Sermon,* Plymouth Congregational Church, Des Moines, IA, February 9, 2014

Barret, Robert L. & Bryan E. Robinson, *Gay Fathers*, Jossey-Bass, A Wiley Company, San Francisco, 2000, p. 104

Boyd, Malcom, *Gay Priest: An Inner Journey*, St. Martin's Press, NY, 1986

Bidstrup, Scott, *At Issue: Gay Marriage*, ISBN15606924, September 1998

Cedar Rapids Gazette, Cedar Rapids, IA, April 14, 2009

Chicago Tribune, April 14, 2009, quoting Associated Press

chicagotribune.com, April 14, 2009

Des Moines Register online, April 14, 2009

Des Moines Register, September 2, 2010, p. 2B

Des Moines Sunday Register, October 28, 2012

Des Moines Sunday Register, September 28, 2014, p. 10P

Des Moines Sunday Register, February 23, 2014, p. 6A

Des Moines Register, October 10, 2014, p. 22A

Faircloth, Sean, *Attack of the Theocrats!: How the Religious Right Harms Us All — and What We Can Do, About It*, Pitchstone Publishing, Charlottesville, Virginia @ 2012, p.52

THE/REPORTER, Grace United Methodist Church Administrative Board, Des Moines, IA, January/February, 2014, p. 5.

Harper, John B. *Facebook page,* August 13, 2013

http://www.youtube.com/watch?v=lmaHqDHTyC8

Interfaith Alliance of Iowa, *Marriage Equality: Myths and Realities,* (brochure)

Kennedy, John F., *Profiles in Courage,* Harper & Brothers, New York, Inaugural Edition 1961, p. 246

Lincoln, Abraham, *Letter to Henry L. Pierce and Others, The Collected Works of ABRAHAM LINCOLN,* Vol. III, Abraham Lincoln Association, Springfield, IL, Roy P. Basler, Editor, Rutgers University Press, New Brunswick, NJ, 1953, p. 376

Lindenberger, Michael A., *Time Magazine,* Saturday, April 04, 2009

Mason City Globe Gazette, Editorial, Mason City, IA, Tuesday, April 21, 2009

Mardis-LeCroy, Matt, Executive Associate Minister (Senior Minister Elect), Plymouth Congregational Church, Des Moines, IA, comments upon receiving the "Protecting Faith and Freedom" Award from the Interfaith Alliance of Iowa, May 21, 2012

Martin, Ricky, *ME,* Celebra, Published by New American Library, a division of Penguin Group [USA], New York, New York, 2010, p. 260-261

Maugham, W. Somerset, *Human Bondage,* International Collectors Library/American Headquarters, Garden City, NY @ 1915, 1936, Doubleday & Co., Inc., p. 19

Miller, Bryce, *Des Moines Register,* April 30, 2013

The New York Times, October 10, 2014, p. EA-22

Obama, President Barack, *Inaugural Address,* January 21, 2013

Olson M.C., Loren A., *Finally Out: Letting Go of Living Straight,* inGroup Press, a division of inGroup Marketing, LLC., 2011, p. 40

Page, Jonathan, ACCESSline, December 2013, p. 26

Public News Service – TN, March 2013

Ross, Alex, *The New Yorker,* November 12, 2012, p. 48

Robinson, Gene, *Episcopal Journal,* August 2012, p. 8

Robinson, Gene, *God Believes in Love: Straight Talk about Gay Marriage,* Alfred A. Knopf, NY, 2012, p. 149

Robinson, Gene, speech Interfaith Alliance of Iowa Awards Dinner, May 2, 2013

Roosevelt, President Franklin D., comments prepared for April 13, 1945

Ruhe, David, Senior Minister, Plymouth Congregational Church, Des Moines, IA

Stephanopoulos, George, *This Week with George Stephanopoulos,* ABC TV, May 31, 2013

Stewart, Jon, *The Daily Show,* April 30, 2013

Strub, Sean, *Body Counts: A Memoir of Politics, AIDS, and Survival*, Scribner, A Division of Simon & Schuster, Inc., NY, NY, 2014

Thompson, Mark, *Gay Soul: Finding the Heart of Gay Spirit and Nature with Sixteen Writers, Healers, Teachers, and Visionaries*, Harper, San Francisco, A Division of Harper Collins Publishers, 1994

Wikipedia, *Same-sex Marriage in the United States*

Wilson, Jonathan, Des Moines Attorney, First Friday Breakfast Club, March 7, 2008

Winters, Dan, *Three Minutes in the Chair*, TV Channel 13, April 14, 2013

CPSIA information can be obtained
at www.ICGtesting.com
Printed in the USA
FFOW05n0256180215